Adam Taki
Spice It Up

First Edition

Library of Congress Control Number: 2012904555
ISBN: 978-0-615-61399-4

Printed in the United States of America

Adam Taki

Spice It Up

100 Tasty, Easy, Healthy Recipes and Food Ideas

Text Jeanne Wolf
Photographer Bobby Quillard
Food Stylist Jeff Parker
Food Scientist Dr. Ghazi Taki

contents

Dedicated to my dad

POTS AND PANS ARE IN MY DNA

My father, Dr. Ghazi Taki (everybody calls him Ghazi), taught me how to love, appreciate, and understand wonderful yet simple food. His ideas and spicy personality are sprinkled throughout this book.

Dad and I have a fan following of Amazing Taste® loyalists. We hear from meat and seafood market managers, professional chefs and directly from consumers. My dad is a true "foodie" *and* a food scientist who always reminds me that I can make everything taste better when I know what I'm doing. Our wish is that you whip out your apron and go on a treasure hunt in your own kitchen. In this book you'll discover new dishes and fresh ideas on many traditional recipes.

You'll also find some well-earned advice about seasoning. Seasoning is what Amazing Taste® is all about. We'll show you how to spice things up in an instant with some tasty tips and ingredients that are easy to find and use. We'll show you that our seasonings can help create a seal around meat so it stays juicy and flavorful.

In the back of the book you'll find some information that will help you be a better, yet safer, cook. With so much talk about "what's good for you," we want you to get more knowledge about eating well, food handling, safety in the kitchen and cooking methods.

When you're thinking, "What's for dinner?" just flip through the pages and get some ideas. Tell us what works for you. (No kidding; that's how we improve.)

Let's have some amazing tastes together.

IT'S OKAY TO PLAY WITH YOUR FOOD

Cooking for me is like playing. I'll tell you why. When I was just three years old I loved to stand at the grill and flip burgers. Okay, it was a toy grill with little plastic burgers, but I also used to like to be near the big, hot "real" grill while my dad was grilling steaks. As I grew older (you know, four and five), I would season my toy steaks and push around my fake chops and get lots and lots of praise. I thought I was cooking and my family gave me tons of compliments about my pretend sensational cuisine.

Those cooking games were a big deal to me because I grew up in a household that enjoyed food and loved spending time in the kitchen. We would entertain family and friends all the time. From the time I was a kid, I associated meals with fun and having people around a table. I thought (and still do think) that dinner was more than dinner if you made it joyous, full of conversation and laughter.

My parents were always very busy so I learned another important thing: I watched them pull a "party" together in a flash. We enjoyed fresh food more than take out or packaged food, but if a dish was a "production" that took a long time to prepare, it wouldn't end up on our table.

My dad's very professional meal planning method was to first open the fridge to take inventory. Then, the menu would become whatever was on the pantry shelves, mixed with whatever fresh vegetables and fruit we had in the kitchen. With very common ingredients, such as chicken, ribs, pasta, rice, leftover sauces or even a dash of ketchup, he always managed to whip up delicious and healthy meals.

I learned by tasting and observing that recipes are just guidelines. That is how you should use this book of meal suggestions and tips.

I confess that even though I cook almost every day, I seldom make the same thing the same way twice. This is a trait I picked up from my father.

Over the years, we've collected and created some recipes that fit the way we cook now. I am sharing with you some well-tested and yummy dishes that you can turn out in a "flash".

The main lesson I learned from my father was that there is no failure in cooking (that is, unless I forget about the pan on the stove when I answer the phone). But seriously, the idea is that a good meal is precious and that preparing one doesn't mean agonizing or buying every odd tool or specialty ingredient you see the chefs use on TV.

With some inspiration from this book, you will be a genius in the kitchen and a very gracious, happy host.

SEASONING FOODS PROPERLY - SPICE IT UP!

Seasoning is an art form but you don't have to be an "artiste" to create every-day masterpieces. Seasoning is what creates the flavor of a dish. You can grow a nice little herb garden and dry or freeze your own fresh herbs and that's a lot of fun. But if you don't have much time to create a gourmet presentation while hungry people are shouting, "When will dinner be ready?" we suggest that you let some experts do the advance work for you.

My father created Amazing Taste® seasonings to let you get just the right taste "instantly". My dad, Dr. Ghazi Taki, has a PhD in Food Science/Meat Science. He has spent his lifetime studying the art of food flavor and making combinations of seasonings that are just about fool proof.

Am I sounding a little "commercial" here? You bet I am! It's the family business and when friends ask, "How did you make that?" often my answer is "With one of our own seasoning packets."

You can gamble a buck (that's right, about a dollar) and try it for yourself. Go to the meat or seafood counter when you are grocery shopping and ask the person in charge to let you taste some of the flavors. Okay...here's a secret. Many of these food professionals use Amazing Taste® seasonings to prepare the best-selling meals they offer in their refrigerated cases.

But that's not all.

The reason these combinations are so great is that they

also act as a seal. You'll be surprised that sprinkling on these magic seasonings will keep your meat, chicken and fish moist and down right juicy.

I love to make turkey burgers in the microwave. I know, you are now picturing a grey mess coming out of the microwave. That would be a waste of good meat and a disappointment to my appetite. When I make my burgers with our seasoning, the moisture doesn't drip or evaporate. I have learned to conquer the microwave. You can also turn out great specialties in the microwave.

The turkey burger trick is the best way I have to show that our stuff works. I mean cooking the burgers in the microwave, not just re-heating. They come out "browned" and good looking. Because of the built-in seal it also is tender, flavorful and evenly cooked. You can count on excellent results every time. You know what to expect. Your burgers and sliders are consistently delicious.

I also have to tell you that Amazing Taste® is relatively low in sodium, contains no MSG, all natural herbs and spices and is the only product I've seen that forms a kind of coating around meat to keep it juicy. If your mouth isn't watering from my description you'll just have to do your own taste test.

The whole idea of this book is to help you find simple, quick, healthy and economical ways to create outstanding meals. One of the best things is how we can show you that you can actually turn out a great feast from the microwave. Let's just admit that microwave cooking (not just reheating) does not have a savory reputation. I am going to show you just how "you-ser" friendly and effective it is.

I haven't held back any of my cooking tips and tricks. There's a lot here that can take the stress out of shopping, planning, and cooking meals.

Cooking has become a national spectator sport. There are so many popular cooking shows! Check out "Spice it Up" and it's your platters people will be watching.

One of the craziest facts I've heard is that most people go shopping and haven't even decided what they are shopping for. Really! They figure out what they are going to serve as they walk up and down the aisles or look for specials in the meat case. If I can help you whip up an impressive meal in a snap, then I'll be happy when you get all the applause.

When you turn out a spiffy meal with ease you will learn to enjoy your own party.

Saying "bon appétit" has kind of been over-used, so let me say, "Go to your kitchen and whip up something **amazing**." Then take a bow.

Hey, you think I said **amazing** enough?

starters

What's a better way to introduce a good meal than with a good appetizer? If what you've put out tastes good, your family gets revved up for the rest of the meal. Anticipation works for food the way it does with other exciting things in life.

Beyond pretzels and olives, here are some taste teasers that are guaranteed to be delicious, speedy, and "you-ser" friendly.

party popcorn

corn kernels*, ½ cup
olive oil, 5 tablespoons
Amazing Taste® Malibu Seasoning, 2 teaspoons

Put corn kernels in a pot and add 3 tablespoons of the olive oil.

Cover and place on MEDIUM heat, leaving the pot lid slightly ajar to allow some steam to escape. Pop for about 4 to 5 minutes or until popping slows.

Place the popped corn into large serving bowl. Drizzle 2 tablespoons of olive oil over the popcorn, tossing to coat evenly. Sprinkle 2 tablespoons of Amazing Taste® Malibu Seasoning over popcorn, and toss again.

You can also do this in a covered dish in the microwave and add Amazing Taste® Malibu Seasoning at the end.

You'll never want to eat any other popcorn again. Serve this and your guests will wonder why they can't get this at your local movie theater concession stand.

No one will notice if you cheat and use microwave popcorn. Just don't pick one that's flavored. You won't want to hide the taste of this.

*Good source of whole grain and fiber.

zesty malibu almonds

raw almonds, 2 cups, whole & blanched
olive oil, 2 teaspoons
Amazing Taste® Malibu Seasoning, 2 teaspoons

Place the almonds in a microwavable dish. Add olive oil and stir. Then, add Amazing Taste® Malibu Seasoning and mix well.

Cook for 2 to 3 minutes on HIGH, stirring once halfway through the cooking.

If they seem a little too oily, blot with a paper towel before you serve. Make plenty. These will go fast...

white bean dip

white kidney beans*, 1 can (15.5 ounces)
garlic powder, 2 teaspoons or use fresh grated garlic
lemon juice, 1 tablespoon
olive oil, 1 tablespoon
Amazing Taste® Malibu Seasoning, 1 teaspoon

Pour the entire contents of the can including liquid into a saucepan
with the garlic powder, lemon juice, olive oil and Amazing Taste® Malibu
Seasoning.

Cook on MEDIUM-HIGH for about 5 minutes.

Transfer mixture from saucepan to food processor or blender, cover, and
blend until smooth.

Transfer dip to serving bowl. Drizzle with olive oil (optional) and sprinkle
with cilantro or parsley. Serve hot or cold with your favorite crackers,
chips or pita bread.

*This is also great with red kidney or garbanzo beans.

18 minutes start to finish
SERVES 4 to 6

california garlic artichoke dip

marinated artichoke hearts, 1 jar (12 ounces), quartered &
marinated or you can use canned (8.5 ounces) unseasoned
artichoke hearts
parmesan cheese, 1 cup, shredded
olive oil, ¼ cup
garlic powder, 1 teaspoon or use grated fresh garlic (but NOT
garlic salt)
Amazing Taste® Malibu Seasoning, 1 tablespoon

Preheat oven to 400°F.

Combine all ingredients, including the liquid, into a food processor or
blender, cover, and blend until smooth.

Pour mixture into a medium-sized baking dish and cover. Bake for 15
minutes.

Serve with chips (different colors and flavors add interest) and crackers,
hot or at room temperature. Small knives or spoons in the dip make it
easy to spread.

eggplant dip

eggplant, 1, medium-sized
tomato, ½ cup
parsley, ½ cup, chopped
onion, ¼ cup, diced
garlic, 1 tablespoon, minced
olive oil, ¼ cup
hot sauce, 1 tablespoon
lemon juice, 1 tablespoon
Amazing Taste® Malibu Seasoning, 1 tablespoon

Preheat the oven to 400°F.

Put all ingredients into a blender or food processor, cover, and blend until the mixture is a smooth consistency but not too liquidy.

Pour into a medium-sized baking dish; cover and cook for 15 minutes.

Serve hot or cold with toasted pita bread, whole wheat crackers or chips of your choice.

For color, sprinkle a tiny amount of paprika on top. Or if your group likes spicy foods, very lightly sprinkle with cayenne pepper.

saucy bloody mary

Amazing Taste® Malibu Seasoning, 1 tablespoon
lime juice, ½ ounce
vodka, 1 ounce (or maybe a half ounce or so more for a little extra kick)
tomato juice, 4 ounces
red hot sauce, 1 tablespoon (just be sure your guests want it extra spicy or you may want to go for a teaspoon)
Worcestershire sauce, 1 dash
celery & green olives to garnish

Put the Amazing Taste® Malibu Seasoning in a small saucer.

Moisten the rim of the highball glass with water or lime juice, turn it upside down and dip it in Amazing Taste® Malibu Seasoning to coat the rim.

Pour ice into glass and, then, add other ingredients along with what remains of the Amazing Taste® Malibu Seasoning in the saucer. Stir three times with a celery stick and garnish with an olive.

Serve and let the good times begin!

If you don't want to use alcohol this still makes a refreshing starter or party drink.

13 minutes start to finish
SERVES 4

avocado chicken sliders

chicken breast, 1 pound, boneless & skinless
Amazing Taste® Chicken Seasoning, 1 packet
ripe avocado, 1
white onion, ½, medium-sized
olive oil, 1 tablespoon
whole wheat rolls, 8, small (about 3 inches in diameter)
cheddar cheese, 8 slices

Cut the chicken breast into strips (about 1 to 2 inches thick) and sprinkle Amazing Taste® Chicken Seasoning on all sides. Cut the avocado into 8 slices. Cut the onion into strips.

Heat a skillet at MEDIUM-HIGH and add olive oil. Sauté the chicken and onion for about 5 minutes, or until the chicken is cooked through.

Place cooked chicken strips and onion on warmed rolls with the cheese and avocado slices on top. You can also serve these open faced.

notes

soups & stews

I have great memories of watching my parents prepare big pots of turkey soup from Thanksgiving leftovers. My dad used to freeze the turkey soup in plastic containers of different sizes for instant use at a later time. Soups are very easy to make! Simply combine your favorite meat, chicken, seafood, vegetables, and beans with the proper liquids, season, and cook to perfection. Soup can be served in small quantities as a first course or could be the main course as we become more interested in healthy eating.

green pea soup

olive oil, 1 tablespoon
onion, ¾ cup, chopped or diced
carrot, ½ cup, chopped
frozen green peas, 1 bag (12 ounces)
beef broth, 1 can (14 ounces), low-sodium
water, 1 cup
Amazing Taste® Beef or Pork Seasoning, 1 packet

In a medium saucepan, heat olive oil and sauté onions on MEDIUM-HIGH for 2 to 3 minutes.

Add chopped carrots, green peas, beef broth, water and 1 packet of Amazing Taste® Beef or Pork Seasoning. Bring to a boil, cover and simmer for 20 minutes.

Put the mixture in a blender. Cover and purée on LOW to avoid splatters.

Garnish with some croutons, a few whole peas and grated cheese for a fancy presentation. To serve as a main course, sauté your favorite sausages, slice and serve on the side.

*This dish goes very well with a heated whole-wheat pita bread used for dipping!

35 minutes start to finish
SERVES 4

chicken fajita soup

chicken breasts, 1 pound, boneless & skinless, cut into small
strips
Amazing Taste® Fajita Seasoning, 1 packet
olive oil, 2 tablespoons
onion, 1 cup, diced
green bell pepper, 1 cup, chopped
tomato, 1 pound, chopped
chicken broth, 14 ounces (1 can), low-sodium
water, 1 cup
fresh lime juice, 3 tablespoons
tortilla chips

Season the chicken strips with ½ the packet of Amazing Taste® Fajita
Seasoning.

In a large soup pot, heat the oil over MEDIUM heat. Add chicken strips,
diced onion, green bell pepper and tomato. Sauté for 6 minutes. Stir
well while cooking.

Add chicken broth, water, lime juice and remaining Amazing Taste®
Fajita Seasoning to the pot, and mix well. Turn up the heat and bring to
a boil.

Reduce the heat, put a cover on the pot and let the soup simmer for 20
to 25 minutes.

Crumble some chips on the top and serve with whole tortilla chips for
dipping.

corn & veggie chowder

olive oil, 1 tablespoon
onion, 1 cup, chopped
frozen sweet corn, 1 bag (12 ounces)
mushroom, 3 cups, chopped
carrot, 1 cup, sliced
tomato, 1 cup, chopped
chicken broth, 1 can (14 ounces), low-sodium (you can also use
vegetable broth)
water, 1 cup
Amazing Taste® Malibu Seasoning, 2 tablespoons

In a medium saucepan, heat the olive oil on MEDIUM-HIGH and sauté
the chopped onion for 2 to 3 minutes. Add all vegetables, broth, water
and the Amazing Taste® Malibu Seasoning. Stir well and bring to a boil.

Cover and simmer for 20 minutes.

Put the mixture in a blender. Cover and purée on LOW to avoid hot
splatters. Serve with toasted bread crumbs or croutons, homemade or
packaged.

1 hour and 30 minutes start to finish
SERVES 4

hearty beef stew

beef stewing meat, 1 pound
Amazing Taste® Beef Seasoning, 1 packet
olive oil, 3 tablespoons
beef broth, 1 can (14 ounces)
water, 1 cup
red potatoes, 8, small, quartered
carrots, 1 cup, cut in 1 inch pieces
celery stalks, 4, cut in 1 inch pieces
onion, 1, medium-sized, sliced

Cut the beef into bite-sized pieces and coat with Amazing Taste® Beef Seasoning.

In a deep, lidded pot, heat the oil on MEDIUM-HIGH heat. Brown the beef well on all sides.

Add beef broth, water, vegetables and remaining Amazing Taste® Beef Seasoning to the pot. Stir the ingredients and bring to a boil.

Reduce the heat and simmer, covered, for 1 hour or until the meat and vegetables are fork tender. Stir occasionally.

Serve over rice, noodles or nestled around a satisfying mound of mashed potatoes.

peppery beef stew

top sirloin steak, 1 pound, trimmed
Amazing Taste® Steak House Seasoning, 1 packet
olive oil, 3 tablespoons
red potatoes, 1 pound (about 4 potatoes), quartered
carrots, 1 cup, cut in 1 inch pieces
celery stalks, 3 (1 cup in all), cut in 1 inch pieces
onion, 1 cup, chopped
beef broth, 1 can (14 ounces), low-sodium
water, 1 cup
cornstarch, dissolved in 2 tablespoons of water

Trim the fat from the top sirloin and cut into 1 inch pieces. Sprinkle Amazing Taste® Steak House Seasoning to cover all sides of the steak and keep the remaining seasoning for later use.

In a large deep, lidded pot, heat the oil on MEDIUM heat. Brown the beef well on all sides – this should take about 5 minutes – stirring constantly.

Add vegetables, beef broth, water and remaining Amazing Taste® Steak House Seasoning to the pot. Stir the ingredients and bring to a boil.

Reduce the heat and simmer. Cover and cook for 45 minutes or until meat and vegetables have that "melt-in-your-mouth" consistency, stirring occasionally. Add dissolved cornstarch and mix well. Continue cooking for 5 minutes.

Serve over rice, noodles or surrounded by mashed potatoes.

1 hour and 30 minutes start to finish
SERVES 4

red potato chicken soup

chicken thighs & drumsticks, 1 pound, skinless
Amazing Taste® Chicken Seasoning, 1 packet
olive oil, 3 tablespoons
red potato, ½ pound, small
carrot, 1 cup, cut in 1 inch pieces
celery stalk, 4, cut in 1 inch pieces
white onion, medium, sliced
chicken broth, 1 can (14 ounces), low-sodium
water, 1 ½ cups

Rinse chicken in cold, running water.

Sprinkle ½ packet of Amazing Taste® Chicken Seasoning on chicken pieces.

In a large deep, lidded pot, heat oil on MEDIUM-HIGH heat and brown chicken pieces well on all sides. Add vegetables, chicken broth, water and remaining Amazing Taste® Chicken Seasoning. Stir and bring to a boil.

Reduce heat to simmer, cover and cook for 1 hour, stirring occasionally, or until the chicken and vegetables are fork tender.

I like to remove the leg bones with tongs before I serve, but the bones give the soup flavor as it cooks so don't just leave them out.

Serve and enjoy! Your guests will think you worked all day. Just sit back and let the compliments roll in.

Everyone needs chicken soup... true comfort food!

notes

salads

Salad brings freshness to any meal. While we all have our own favorite salad, we always make new tasting salads depending on what we have on hand in the refrigerator. Also, by adding high protein ingredients such as beef, poultry, seafood, cheese and hard-boiled eggs, you can turn a salad into a satisfying, nutritious main course.

all-american potato salad

potatoes, 1 pound (4 to 5), medium-sized
bacon, 3-4 slices
onion, ½ cup, finely-chopped
celery, ½ cup, finely, chopped
parsley, ½ cup, finely-chopped
mayonnaise, ½ cup
yellow mustard, 1 tablespoon
milk, ½ cup
Amazing Taste® Malibu Seasoning, 1 tablespoon

Peel the potatoes and boil them for 12 to 16 minutes or until just tender. Drain the potatoes. Cut into ¾ inch cubes.

While boiling the potatoes, cook the bacon slices in a small frying pan. Cook until crispy. Remove and chop into very small pieces.

In a large bowl, combine onion, celery and parsley, and add the chopped potatoes.

In a small bowl, mix the mayonnaise, mustard, milk and the Amazing Taste® Malibu Seasoning. Blend very well and add to the potato mixture.

Toss gently. Serve and enjoy.

white bean salad

white kidney beans, 1 can (15.5 ounces)
green onion, ½ cup, chopped
green bell pepper, ½ cup, chopped finely
tomato, ½ cup, chopped finely
parsley, ½ cup, chopped
white vinegar, ¼ cup
olive oil, ¼ cup
Amazing Taste® Malibu Seasoning, 1 tablespoon
eggs, 2, hard-boiled

In a small pot, bring the beans to a boil in their liquid and cook for 2 minutes. Remove from heat. Drain and cool in the refrigerator.

Add vegetables to beans and mix gently. Separately, combine the white vinegar, olive oil and Amazing Taste® Malibu Seasoning. Mix well and pour over the bean mixture.

Garnish each plate with half a slice of the hard-boiled egg and green onions if desired.

ghazi's fresh mint salad

cucumber, 1 cup, peeled & sliced
carrots, 1 cup, peeled & sliced
red cabbage, 1 cup, shredded
onion (white or red), 1 cup, chopped
tomato, 1 cup, sliced
fresh mint, 1 cup, chopped
Amazing Taste® Malibu Seasoning, 2 tablespoons
hot sauce, 2 tablespoons
lemon juice, ¼ cup
olive oil, ¼ cup

Combine cucumbers, carrots, cabbage, onion, tomato and mint in a large bowl and mix. Add Amazing Taste® Malibu Seasoning, hot sauce, lemon juice and olive oil. Mix well and serve!

shrimp fajita salad

olive oil, ½ cup
raw shrimp, 1 pound, peeled & deveined
Amazing Taste® Fajita Seasoning, 1 packet
romaine lettuce, 4 cups, chopped
bell pepper, 1 cup, 1-inch slices
onion, 1 cup, sliced
tomato, 1 cup, sliced
ripe avocado, 2
lemon juice, ¼ cup

Preheat a large skillet over MEDIUM heat, dropping in ¼ cup of olive oil.

Season the shrimp with 1 tablespoon of Amazing Taste® Fajita Seasoning and mix well. Sauté the shrimp for 4 to 5 minutes in a preheated skillet, turning constantly until the shrimp turns orange in color and are just cooked. Set aside.

In a large bowl, mix lettuce, bell pepper, onion and tomato. Toss well and divide the salad mix evenly into four serving dishes.

Cut each halved avocado into thirds. You will have 12 slices. Arrange 3 slices of the avocado on each serving dish around the salad mixture.

Divide the shrimp into four portions and place them on top of the salads.

In a measuring cup, mix the remaining Amazing Taste® Fajita Seasoning with the rest of the olive oil and ¼ cup lemon juice. Drizzle the dressing over the salad (about 2 tablespoons on each salad or to taste). Serve and enjoy!

It's a good idea to make some extra dressing on the side. After all, everyone *will* ask for more.

turkey chili salad

ground turkey, 1 pound, lean
Amazing Taste® Chili Seasoning, 1 packet
olive oil, 2 tablespoons
lettuce, 1 medium-sized head, chopped
red onion, 1, medium-sized, sliced
tomato, 1, chopped
green bell pepper, 1, cored, seeded & chopped
cheddar cheese, 1 cup, shredded (or use mixed, shredded Mexican style cheese)
tortilla chips, 1 bag, 7 ounces, crumbled

Season the ground turkey with Amazing Taste® Chili Seasoning and mix well.

In a large skillet, heat olive oil on MEDIUM-HIGH. Add seasoned ground turkey and stir until crumbly and no longer pink.

Combine the lettuce, red onion, tomato and bell pepper in a large salad bowl and add the cooked turkey chili. Toss salad and top with crumbled tortilla chips and cheese.

beach bbq salad

chicken breast, 1 pound, boneless & skinless
Amazing Taste® Chicken Seasoning, 1 tablespoon
olive oil, 1 tablespoon
romaine lettuce, 1 bag (or 1 head of lettuce cut crosswise into thin strips)
corn, 1 can (15 ounces), drained, low-sodium & whole kernel
black beans, 1 can (15 ounces), drained, low-sodium
ripe avocado, 1, halved, pitted, peeled & sliced
bbq sauce, ¼ cup of your favorite kind
ranch dressing (to taste)
cilantro, 2 tablespoons

Cut the chicken breasts into 1 to 2 inch thick strips and coat all sides with Amazing Taste® Chicken Seasoning.

Heat the olive oil in a large skillet on MEDIUM heat, add the seasoned chicken strips and sauté for 5 minutes or until no longer pink.

Place the lettuce in a large serving bowl. Drain the corn and beans and add them to the lettuce. Slice the avocado and add to the mixture as well.

Top the salad with the fully-cooked chicken. Add as much BBQ sauce and ranch dressing as you like, but don't mask the natural tastes of the ingredients with too much flair!

Toss salad and sprinkle cilantro to taste, if desired, and serve!

notes

beef

Beef recipes are a part of my collection that I regularly cook and enjoy. They have endured the test of time and certain alterations make them classics for today. I know this because friends, family, and Amazing Taste® customers are always asking for tips and ideas.

My doctor-of-food science father taught me that kids, as well as adults, need to make sure that they include protein-heavy meals in their daily diets. Beef, when used in moderation, is the perfect go-to source for protein. Additionally, beef is an excellent source for iron, zinc, B vitamins, especially B-6 and B-12, and niacin. These essential nutrients provide energy, develop muscles and bones, and build strong immune systems.

There are times when nothing but beef will do for me. I love a great steak, a juicy burger and the wide array of dishes you can make with beef.

By the way, there is an ongoing discussion about which hamburger meat is best. Some say ground sirloin; others say ground chuck. We have found that, in most cases, what they just call "hamburger meat" is best. Stores are much more careful and open about fat and other ingredients in the meat nowadays. There are usually people in the meat department at your favorite supermarket who can help you sort it out. Even when on a diet, you don't want burgers to be too dry. Remember, a lot of fat drips out as you cook the meat.

fiesta burger

ground beef, 1 pound
onions, ¼ cup, finely chopped
jalapeño peppers, ½ cup, fresh, chopped & seeds removed*
garlic cloves, 2, minced (or you can use a garlic press)
oregano flakes, 1 teaspoon, dried
tomato sauce or salsa, 2 ounces
Amazing Taste® Burger Seasoning, 1 tablespoon
whole wheat buns, 4, split

Combine all ingredients (except Amazing Taste® Burger Seasoning and buns) together in a shallow dish.

Shape the mixture into 4 patties and coat well with Amazing Taste® Burger Seasoning.

Broil, grill or BBQ for 5 to 6 minutes on each side (or until desired doneness).

Layer the buns with your favorite condiments (such as lettuce, a slice of tomato, onions and avocado). For a more "fiesta" flavor, add more jalapeño peppers or salsa. I like to spread some mayonnaise on the buns as well.

*It's a good idea to wear food preparation gloves while handling hot peppers.

southwest burger

black beans, 1 can (15 ounces), reduced-sodium, drained
ground beef, 1 pound
Amazing Taste® Chili Seasoning, 1 packet
whole wheat buns, 6
salsa or pico de gallo, ¾ cup
avocado, 2, halved, pitted & sliced

Drain liquid from black beans. Mix together beans, ground beef, and
Amazing Taste® Chili Seasoning. Form 6 patties from the mixture.

Grill the patties over MEDIUM heat for 4 to 5 minutes on each side until
done (beef should reach a minimum internal temperature of 160°F and
turkey should reach 165°F).

Place each patty on a bun and cover with salsa and avocado slices.
Extra goodies: sliced tomato, grilled onion, chopped scallions, shredded
or grated cheese, sour cream, etc.

steak house burger

ground beef, 1 pound
Amazing Taste® Steak House Seasoning, 1 tablespoon
whole wheat buns, 4
tomato, 1 medium-sized, sliced
onion, 1 medium-sized, sliced
lettuce (iceberg), 4 leaves
cheddar cheese, 4 slices

Form the ground beef in ¼ pound burger patties and sprinkle Amazing Taste® Steak House Seasoning to cover the patties well on all sides.

Grill the patties to desired doneness (they should reach a minimum internal temperature of 160°F). Toast the buns and layer with lettuce, beef, tomato, onion, lettuce cheese – along with any other toppings you may want – and serve.

Sweet potato wedges (on page 123) are great with this burger!

Want to lose the buns and help slim yours? Layer whole lettuce leaves on a platter (butter lettuce works best). Make your own burger lettuce wraps. Messy, but good for you, and fun to eat.

gourmet burger

ground beef, 1 pound
green onions, ¼ cup, chopped
parsley, ¼ cup, minced
garlic cloves, 2, minced
soy sauce, 3 tablespoons, low-sodium
mustard, 1 teaspoon
Worcestershire sauce, 1 teaspoon
Amazing Taste® Burger Seasoning, 1 tablespoon
whole wheat buns, 4

Combine all ingredients (except Amazing Taste® Burger Seasoning and buns) together in a shallow dish. Mix everything well, making sure to separate any clumps of vegetables.

Shape the mixture into 4 round patties and coat well with Amazing Taste® Burger Seasoning on both sides.

Broil or grill each patty for 5 to 6 minutes on each side (or until desired doneness). If you want to test the doneness of the meat, insert a meat thermometer into its center to ensure that it's at least 160°F.

Layer the buns with your favorite condiments (lettuce, tomato slices, onion, etc.) and serve!

1 hour and 20 minutes start to finish
SERVES 4

stuffed bell peppers

brown rice (dry), ½ cup
water, 1 ½ cups
red bell peppers, 4, large
ground beef, ½ pound
onion, ½ cup, finely chopped
marinara sauce, 1 cup
Worcestershire sauce, 1 tablespoon
Amazing Taste® Malibu Seasoning, 1 tablespoon
olive oil, 2 teaspoons

Combine the rice and water in a saucepan and bring to a boil. Reduce heat to MEDIUM-LOW and cover. Simmer for 30 minutes or until water is absorbed.

While the rice is cooking, rinse the bell peppers, slice the tops off and remove the membranes and the seeds. Cook the ground beef and onion in a pan over MEDIUM heat for approximately 5 to 6 minutes or until the meat is no longer pink.

Preheat oven to 350°F.

In a large bowl, thoroughly mix together the cooked rice, cooked ground beef and onion, ¾ cup marinara sauce (saving the remaining sauce to top stuffed peppers), Worcestershire sauce and Amazing Taste® Malibu Seasoning. Spoon the mixture into bell peppers and place them in a lightly oiled baking dish. Spread the remaining marinara sauce over the bell peppers.

Cover with foil and bake in oven for about 35 minutes or until they are hot throughout. Remove the foil cover during the last 10 minutes of baking. Sprinkle the baked peppers with grated cheese, if desired, and serve hot. White rice may be substituted for brown rice in this recipe.

beef & macaroni

water, 2 quarts
elbow macaroni, 2 cups
olive oil, 2 tablespoons
ground beef, 1 pound
onion, 1 cup, chopped
tomatoes, 1 cup, chopped
Amazing Taste® Malibu Seasoning, 1 packet
parsley, 2 tablespoons, chopped
parmesan cheese, 1 cup, shredded

In a medium-sized pot, bring 2 quarts (64 ounces) of water to a boil.

Add the macaroni and boil gently, uncovered, for approximately 8 to 10 minutes, stirring frequently*. While your pasta is cooking, prepare the rest of your dish.

In a large skillet, heat the olive oil on MEDIUM-HIGH and add ground beef, onion, tomatoes and Amazing Taste® Malibu Seasoning. Cook for approximately 5 minutes (or until meat is cooked thoroughly and no longer pink).

Check your macaroni for doneness by taking a piece and chewing it. Just be careful not to burn your fingers or mouth. Drain the macaroni and pour it, along with the parsley and cheese, into the beef and vegetable mixture. Continue cooking on MEDIUM until the cheese melts. Serve and enjoy!

*If you prefer your pasta a bit on the firmer side, or, al dente, boil for only 5 or 6 minutes.

beef eggplant parmesan

olive oil, ¼ cup
eggplant, 1, large, sliced ¼ inch thick
Amazing Taste® Burger Seasoning, 1 packet
ground beef, 1 pound
onion, 1 cup, chopped
tomatoes, 1 ½ cups, chopped
tomato sauce, 1 can (8 ounces), no salt added
garlic powder, 1 tablespoon (or minced garlic)
parmesan cheese, 1 cup, grated

Brush the surface of a large baking dish with 2 tablespoons of olive oil and arrange the slices of eggplant.

Heat a frying pan on MEDIUM and add the remaining olive oil. Mix together the Amazing Taste® Burger Seasoning with the ground beef. Sauté the seasoned beef and onions for about 4 minutes (until the onions are slightly translucent).

When ready, evenly spread the meat and onion mixture over the eggplant slices and top with chopped tomatoes and tomato sauce.

Sprinkle garlic powder and parmesan cheese on top – add more if you're a cheese fiend! – and then bake for about 25 minutes until the eggplant is done and tender to the touch of a fork.

beef chili pizza

olive oil, 2 tablespoons
ground beef, 1 pound
onion, 1 cup, medium-sized, chopped
red bell pepper, medium-sized, cut into ½ inch strips
tomato, 1 cup, sliced
Amazing Taste® Chili Seasoning, 1 packet
pizza crust*, 12 inch
shredded cheese, 1 cup
cilantro, 2 tablespoons, fresh, stemmed & chopped (optional)

Preheat oven to 425°F.

In a large skillet, heat oil on MEDIUM. Add the ground beef, onion, bell pepper, and Amazing Taste® Chili Seasoning and mix well. Brown the beef for 6 minutes or until it's no longer pink. The seasoning and onions will make your kitchen smell great.

Place the prepared pizza crust on a large lightly-oiled baking sheet. Sprinkle half the cheese on top of the crust. Add the beef, vegetable mixture, and sliced tomato, and then top with the remaining cheese.

Bake until the cheese is melted and the crust is crispy (this should only take about 15 minutes).

To serve, sprinkle with cilantro, if desired, and cut into 8 wedges. You can offer more chili fixings like chopped onion or sour cream on the side. Use your imagination!

*There are a lot of choices when it comes to pizza crust. The frozen pizza crusts are fine and you can also get frozen pizza dough and knead it into a crust yourself. Also, you can make a good pizza using pita bread.

15 minutes start to finish
SERVES 6

speedy chili

ground beef or turkey, 1 pound
water, ½ cup
Amazing Taste® Chili Seasoning, 1 packet
tomatoes, 1 can (14.5 ounces) diced, or tomato sauce, 2 cans (8 ounces each)
kidney or pinto beans, 1 can (15.5 ounces)

Brown the ground beef in a large skillet on MEDIUM heat. (If using ground turkey, heat a little olive oil in the skillet when cooking.) Add water, Amazing Taste® Chili Seasoning, undrained tomatoes or tomato sauce and beans. Stir well.

Bring mixture to a boil. Cover, reduce heat and simmer for 10 minutes, stirring occasionally.

Ladle the chili into serving bowls and offer shredded cheese, chopped onions, sour cream, chopped olives, minced jalapeño peppers, chopped fresh cilantro and sliced avocado on the side. Allow each diner to add their choice of toppings. (Don't be afraid to experiment.)

8 minutes start to finish
SERVES 4

southwestern scramble

Amazing Taste® Beef Seasoning, 1 packet
ground beef, 1 pound
olive oil, 2 tablespoons
eggs, 4, beaten
beans, 1 can (15.5 ounces), drained
salsa, 1 cup (your choice of mildness)
cilantro, 1 tablespoon, fresh, stemmed & chopped (optional)

Mix the Amazing Taste® Beef Seasoning with the ground beef and set it aside.

In a large skillet, heat olive oil on MEDIUM-HIGH and brown the seasoned meat. Meanwhile, beat the four eggs together. Add the beans and salsa. Mix well for the best consistency.

Add the egg mixture to the browned beef and cook, stirring constantly to avoid burning, until all of the ingredients are cooked through.

Sprinkle with cilantro, if desired, and serve. Cilantro adds a unique taste dimension. This dish is so versatile that it may be served for breakfast, lunch or dinner.

*My bean of choice for this dish is white pinto. Not only does it add a nice contrast in color and texture, but pinto beans are extremely versatile.

pepper steak stir-fry

sirloin steak, 1 pound, cut into 1 inch strips
Amazing Taste® Beef Seasoning, 1 packet
olive oil, 2 tablespoons
green bell pepper, 1, cut into strips*
red bell pepper, 1, cut into strips*
onion, ½, white, medium-sized, cut into strips*
baby bella mushrooms, ½ pound, sliced

Sprinkle the beef using ¼ of the Amazing Taste® Beef Seasoning packet, coating all strips well.

Heat the olive oil in a large skillet on MEDIUM and sauté the beef for about 4 minutes, giving the surface of the meat an even, brown color.

Add bell peppers, onion, mushrooms, and remaining Amazing Taste® Beef Seasoning, and continue to cook for another 2 minutes.

When the veggies are cooked and the onions seem translucent, serve your dish! (I prefer to serve my stir-fry over brown rice or whole wheat noodles.)

*Save time and pick up pre-sliced and washed vegetables in your grocer's fresh produce department!

amazing steaks

steak (porterhouse, strip, tenderloin, or sirloin), 4, ¾ - 1 inch thick

marinade:
coarse black pepper, 2 teaspoons
olive oil, ¼ cup
red wine, ¼ cup (you can also use water or beef broth!)
soy sauce, 2 tablespoons
Worcestershire sauce, 1 tablespoon
Amazing Taste® Beef Seasoning, 1 packet

Combine all marinade ingredients and mix well.

Place your steaks in a shallow pan and pour the marinade mixture over them. Turn the steaks over so you can cover both sides with the marinade. Then, pierce the steaks with a fork to allow the juices to seep into the meat for fuller flavor.

Marinate for at least 15 minutes or, if you want a more intense flavor, cover the steak and put it in the refrigerator to soak in the marinade for a few hours.

Broil, grill or BBQ the steaks for approximately 5 to 7 minutes on each side (or until desired doneness which is where that meat thermometer comes in handy), basting with the marinade while cooking.

When you've checked for proper doneness, serve and you'll be soaking up raves for that unique taste. Don't forget to discard any remaining marinade.

This steak is pictured with sauteed mushrooms (recipe on page 127).

rib-eye steak dinner

rib-eye steak, 2, 1 inch thick (6-8 ounces each)
Amazing Taste® Steak House Seasoning, 1 packet
olive oil, ¼ cup
mushrooms, ½ cup, sliced
red wine, ¼ cup

Sprinkle Amazing Taste® Steak House Seasoning on the steak, covering both sides.

Grill over MEDIUM heat, until desired doneness, flipping once. This should take about 10 to 12 minutes to cook to medium doneness.   Of course, you can also use your oven broiler.

In a large skillet, heat the olive oil on MEDIUM heat. Add the sliced mushrooms, red wine and the remaining Amazing Taste® Steak House Seasoning. Cook until the mushrooms are tender.

Place mushrooms on top of the steaks and serve.   The mushrooms add a little extra eye appeal and they taste great. If you want to take this dish to another level try it with Ghazi's Fresh Mint Salad (page 37).

garlic grilled tri-tip

Worcestershire sauce, ½ cup
olive oil, ½ cup
garlic, 2 tablespoons, minced
Amazing Taste® Beef Seasoning (or, for a bolder flavor, try
Amazing Taste® Steak House Seasoning), 1 packet
tri-tip roast or roast tenderloin, 2 - 2 ½ pounds

Combine Worcestershire sauce, olive oil, minced garlic and Amazing Taste® Beef Seasoning. Mix thoroughly.

Put the meat in a deep glass dish and pour marinade evenly across the surface. Flip the meat so you're sure to evenly cover all sides with the marinade. Pierce the meat all over with a fork so the mixture will seep under the surface and into the center as well.

Put the dish in the refrigerator for 15 minutes or longer to marinate. The longer you leave it, the more intense the flavor will be!

If you are using a gas grill, turn the heat to MEDIUM and heat the grill's surface first. If you are using charcoal, spread the coals to form a slope, light the charcoal, and let the coals settle to a nice MEDIUM heat. Grill until desired doneness, turning once. If you don't have a grill, use your oven broiler.

This is great tailgate party food served with small ciabatta bread rolls and All-American Potato Salad (page 35) on the side.

standing rib roast

beef rib roast, 1 (3 ½ - 4 pounds)
beef broth, ½ cup, low-sodium
Worcestershire sauce, ¼ cup
prepared horseradish, ¼ cup
Dijon mustard, ¼ cup
garlic powder, 2 tablespoons
Amazing Taste® Steak House Seasoning, 1 packet

Preheat the oven to 450°F. Place the roast, fatty side up, in a shallow-sided roasting rack.

In a small bowl, combine the beef broth, Worcestershire sauce, horseradish, Dijon mustard, garlic powder and Amazing Taste Steak House Seasoning and mix together thoroughly into a thick marinade.

Cover the roast with your marinade, working it in to all the nooks and crannies of the meat to ensure fullest flavor.

Roast the meat for 25 minutes at 450°F. Then, reduce heat to 350°F and continue roasting for about 45 minutes until the internal temperature is at 145°F for medium rare. When checking, push a meat thermometer into a spot that will allow it to penetrate to the center of the roast.

Transfer the roast to a platter and let stand for 10 or 15 minutes. Carve and serve with a yummy assortment of potatoes and veggies.

dutch pot roast

beef chuck roast, 1 (about 2 ½ pounds)
Amazing Taste® Beef Seasoning, 1 packet
olive oil, 2 tablespoons
beef broth, 1 can (14 ounces), low-sodium
onion, 1, medium-sized, cut into halves (about ½ inch thick)
tomato sauce, 1 can (8 ounces), no salt added
celery stalks, 3, cut into 1 inch pieces
carrots, 2, regular-sized, cut into 1 inch pieces
potatoes, 2, large, peeled & quartered
rosemary, 3, fresh sprigs, minced
garlic cloves, 4, minced (try a garlic press)

Coat the entire roast with about ½ packet of Amazing Taste® Beef Seasoning.

In a large pot or Dutch oven*, add olive oil and heat to MEDIUM-HIGH.

Place roast into the pot and sear the meat for about 2 ½ minutes on each side. Make sure than each side is browned nicely.

Add water or beef broth and bring to a boil. Then reduce the heat and cook.

Add onions, tomato sauce, beef broth, celery, carrots, potatoes, rosemary, garlic and the rest of the Amazing Taste® Beef Seasoning to the pot. Stir and bring to a boil. Reduce the heat and cook for 1 to 2 hours until the meat and vegetables are fork tender. I always taste as I go.

* After searing roast, you can also use a slow cooker instead of cooking on the stove.

beef kabobs

top sirloin steak, 1 pound, cut into chunks
onion, 1, cut into wedges
bell peppers, 3, any color, medium-sized, cut into 1 inch squares
cherry tomatoes, 4
mushrooms, 4, small & whole
olive oil, 2 tablespoons
Amazing Taste® Steak House Seasoning, 1 packet

additional items:
wood or metal skewers *

Thread your ingredients on to the skewers and drizzle the kabobs evenly with olive oil. Then, sprinkle all sides of the meat and vegetables generously with Amazing Taste® Steak House Seasoning.

Heat your grill to MEDIUM-HIGH heat and cook the kabobs 6 to 8 minutes per side until desired doneness.

Serve with your favorite rice dish on the side. Try Mushroom Rice Pilaf (on page 128) or Mediterranean Rice (on page 129) on the side or inside of some pita bread that's topped with Ghazi's Mint Salad (on page 37).

* If you're using wooden skewers, be sure to soak them in water for 10 minutes so they don't burn. You want the kabob to have the smoky taste, not the stick.

bloody mary marinated beef ribs

bloody mary mix, ½ cup liquid (and you thought it was just for a cocktail)
Amazing Taste® Beef Seasoning, 1 packet
beef back ribs, 2 pounds

Preheat your oven to 300°F.

In a bowl, combine bloody mary mix and Amazing Taste® Beef Seasoning and mix well.

Place ribs on a tray and coat with the marinade. Put the tray in the oven and bake until the internal temperature checked with your trusty meat thermometer is at least at 165°F.

If you want to prepare ahead of time and for optimum flavor, soak the ribs, covered, in the refrigerator. Just smile when someone asks, "How did you get that taste?"

notes

poultry

Poultry is good for you... it ranks high among healthy foods and is an excellent source of protein, niacin, vitamin B-6, B-12, phosphorous and zinc. Though poultry does contain fat, saturated fat and cholesterol, most of it is in the skin. To reduce calories and fat, just remove the skin after cooking.

White meat? Dark meat? Wings? Legs? Everybody has their favorites in the poultry category. Fried chicken is comfort food for some; Duck à l'Orange is a rare gourmet treat. (At my house we rub the duck with Amazing Taste® and add orange juice to the sauce and the basting juice and we call it a fancy supper. You just try to say "Duck à l'Orange" to a bunch of hungry kids.)

I've substituted pounded chicken breasts for veal and I love my turkey burgers. I recently came across ground turkey meat from only the dark parts of the turkey and I found that it makes a delicious switch from my everyday turkey burgers and sliders. When I know what everybody likes, I'll sometimes buy extra chicken or turkey parts so everyone gets exactly what they want.

I suppose you could say that poultry is the chameleon of meats! Poultry can adapt to all culture styles or taste choices. Those birds can star in just about any role you could want in a main course or as a starter. They're very compatible, too. You can surround them with fruit, veggies or potatoes and make a meal in a pan and they won't make a peep.

From now on when your family asks, "Chicken for dinner?" you'll reply, "Which one of my fabulous poultry dishes would you like?"

Poultry is usually pretty kind to the cook if the cook treats it tenderly. Poultry needs spice, moisture, and to be tested with a thermometer for proper cooking time. Anyone who longs for a turkey sandwich from the Thanksgiving left-overs can tell you that poultry can be good hot, cold, made into a salad, with dressing on or even very plain. Cornish hens follow the same rules. But those little chickens can look very festive on a platter. At our house, we fall back on hens for birthday dinners and company "show-off" meals.

anna's enchiladas

chicken breast, 2 pounds, boneless & skinless
olive oil, 2 tablespoons
Amazing Taste® Chicken Seasoning, 1 packet
green chilies, 1 can (7 ounces), diced
sour cream, 2 cups (16 ounces)
monterey jack cheese, 2 cups, shredded
cream of chicken soup, 3 cans (31.5 ounces), 98% fat free
flour tortillas, 12

Preheat oven to 350°F.

Lightly coat chicken breasts with olive oil and use any remaining oil to coat the bottom of a medium-sized baking pan. Coat all sides of the chicken with Amazing Taste® Chicken Seasoning.

Place seasoned chicken in the pan and bake for 40 minutes or until it reaches an internal temperature of 165°F.

While chicken is baking, mix green chilies, sour cream and chicken soup in a bowl and set aside.

Remove chicken from oven and let it cool for about 5 minutes. When chicken is cool enough to handle, chop the chicken into bite-sized pieces.

Lightly grease a casserole dish that's large enough to hold the enchiladas.

Spread 2 to 3 tablespoons of the soup mixture evenly covering the bottom of a casserole dish. Assemble the enchiladas by placing approximately 1 tablespoon of soup mixture, a pinch of cheese and 2 tablespoons of chicken in the center of each tortilla. Roll up and place seam side down in the casserole dish.

Once all the enchiladas are in the dish, spread the remaining soup mixture over the enchiladas and top with remaining cheese.

Bake at 350°F for about 20 minutes or until cooked through.

Wait a couple of minutes before serving. It really does give all the flavors a chance to blend together.

chicken fajita pizza

chicken breast, 2 (1 pound), boneless & skinless
Amazing Taste® Fajita Seasoning, 1 packet
pizza crust, 12-inch, thin (there are many varieties to choose
from including refrigerated and frozen - you can also use frozen
pizza dough and knead it into a crust yourself)
onion, 1, medium-sized, cut into thin strips
green bell pepper, 1, medium-sized
olive oil, 2 tablespoons
pizza sauce, ½ cup (or use tomato sauce with a little oregano)
shredded jack or cheddar cheese, ½ cup
cilantro (optional), 1 tablespoon, stemmed & chopped

Preheat the oven to 425°F.

Cut the chicken breast into bite-sized pieces and coat with Amazing
Taste® Fajita Seasoning.

Heat oil in a large skillet on MEDIUM heat. Add seasoned chicken,
onion and bell peppers, and sauté. Stir frequently until the chicken
browns on all sides and is cooked throughout. This should take
approximately 5 minutes.

Spread the pizza sauce on the crust. Top the crust with chicken,
vegetables and cheese.

Bake on a dry, ungreased cookie sheet for about 15 minutes, or until the
crust is crisp and the cheese is fully melted. Sprinkle with cilantro, if
desired, and serve!

artichoke chicken

chicken breast, 1 pound, boneless & skinless
Amazing Taste® Chicken Seasoning, 1 packet
olive oil, 1 tablespoon
artichoke hearts, 1 can or jar (12 ounces), marinated
green onions, 1 cup, chopped
mushrooms, ½ pound, sliced
garlic powder, ¼ teaspoon
oregano flakes, ¼ teaspoon, dry
chicken broth, ½ cup, low-sodium

Cut chicken breasts into 1 to 2 inch strips.

Sprinkle ½ packet of Amazing Taste® Chicken Seasoning on the strips, toss and coat evenly on both sides.

In a large skillet, add olive oil and heat on MEDIUM. Add seasoned chicken strips and sauté for about 5 minutes or until browned. Add all remaining ingredients, including the rest of the Amazing Taste® Chicken Seasoning to the browned chicken and stir. Continue to cook for about 2 minutes.

This goes great with pasta or your choice of rice. See pages 128 and 129 for two delicious rice-based recipes!

20 minutes start to finish
SERVES 4

ginger chicken & vegetables

chicken breast, 1 pound, boneless & skinless, cut into 1 inch strips
Amazing Taste® Chicken Seasoning, ½ packet
olive oil, 2 tablespoons
broccoli florets, 3 ½ cups
carrots, 1 cup, sliced
snow peas, ¾ cup
soy sauce, ¼ cup, low-sodium
garlic powder or minced garlic, 1 teaspoon
ginger root, 1 tablespoon (fresh grated ginger has more flavor power than powdered - you can also use pickled, sliced ginger, a popular condiment for sushi)

Sprinkle the chicken breast strips with ½ packet of Amazing Taste® Chicken Seasoning, coating all sides well and reserve remaining Seasoning in packet for later use in the recipe.

Heat olive oil in a wok or large pan on MEDIUM-HIGH heat. Add the seasoned chicken and sauté for about 3 minutes.

Add all vegetables and remaining ingredients, including the remaining Amazing Taste® Chicken Seasoning. Continue cooking for 4 to 5 minutes. You don't want the vegetables to lose their crunch.

Serve over a bed of white or brown rice or try rice noodles.

lime grilled chicken

marinade:
fresh lime juice, ½ cup (about 2 limes)
olive oil, 3 tablespoons
lime zest, 1 teaspoon, grate using the small side of the grater
Amazing Taste® Chicken Seasoning, 1 packet

chicken breast, 4, boneless & skinless

Combine all of the marinade ingredients and mix well. Marinate the chicken for at least 15 minutes at room temperature or, for deeper flavor, let the chicken sit in the marinade, refrigerator, for a couple of hours or overnight. When ready to cook, take the marinated chicken out of the refrigerator.

Heat the grill to MEDIUM-HIGH and place the marinated breast on the grill. Cook, basting periodically, for 6 minutes on each side or until chicken is tender and the meat is no longer pink. The internal temperature should be at least 165°F. Discard the remaining marinade.

Serve with your favorite vegetables or a nice salad!

30 minutes start to finish
SERVES 4

mediterranean chicken

chicken breast, 2, boneless & skinless
Amazing Taste® Chicken Seasoning, 1 packet
olive oil, 2 tablespoons
onion, 1 cup, diced
red bell pepper, 1 cup, diced
eggplant, 2 cups, diced (bite-sized)
zucchini, 2 cup, diced (bite-sized)
tomato, 1 can (14.5 ounces), peeled & diced, no-salt added
garlic cloves, 2, chopped

Pound the 4 chicken breast pieces flat. Pounding meat is easy with plastic wrap on both sides, or you can put your meat in a Ziploc bag. Pound the meat with a kitchen mallet or whatever heavy object works for you!

Coat the chicken with Amazing Taste® Chicken Seasoning. Heat the olive oil in a large skillet and sauté the chicken on MEDIUM-HIGH heat. After cooking the chicken for about 2 minutes on each side, add the onion, red bell pepper, eggplant, zucchini, tomato and garlic.

Sauté all the ingredients together for another 3 or 4 minutes, or until the onions become translucent, and serve.

shredded chicken cacciatore

Amazing Taste® Chicken Seasoning, 1 packet
chicken breasts, 2 (1 pound), boneless & skinless
olive oil, 3 tablespoons
chicken broth, 1 can (14 ounces), low-sodium
onion, 1 cup, chopped
celery, 1 cup, chopped
bell pepper, 1 cup, chopped
carrot, 1 cup, thinly sliced
mushroom, 1 cup, thinly sliced
red or white wine, ½ cup (optional)
hot sauce, 1 teaspoon (optional)

Sprinkle Amazing Taste® Chicken Seasoning on both sides of the
chicken breasts, coating well. Keep the remaining seasoning for later
use. In a large, lidded pot, heat the olive oil on MEDIUM-HIGH heat.
Add seasoned chicken and brown the meat for 2 to 3 minutes on each
side.

Add broth, vegetables, the remaining to Amazing Taste® Chicken
Seasoning, wine and hot sauce, and mix well. Stir and bring the mixture
to a boil. Cover, and reduce the heat and simmer for 1 hour or until the
chicken is tender enough to be shredded.

Place the chicken breasts on a cutting board, and shred with two forks
into bite-sized pieces. Return the chicken to the pot, stir and cook for
and additional 2 to 3 minutes.

Serve with rice, pasta or toasted bread with a dash of olive oil.

1 hour and 45 minutes start to finish
SERVES 4

spicy stuffed rotisserie chicken

chicken, 4-5 pounds, whole
Amazing Taste® Chicken Seasoning, 1 packet

vegetable stuffing:
butter, 3 tablespoons (reserve 1 tablespoon for later use)
onion, 1 cup, diced
celery, 4 sticks, chopped into ½ inch pieces
carrots, 4, chopped into ½ inch pieces
mushrooms (baby bellas), ¾ cup, sliced
thyme, ½ tablespoon, dry
basil, ½ tablespoon, dry
hot sauce, 2 tablespoons (optional)

Chicken:

Preheat oven to 375°F.

Rinse the chicken in cold water and clean out the cavity. Pat it dry
with a paper towel and sprinkle the cavity with Amazing Taste® Chicken
Seasoning, reserving the rest of the packet for later use.

Vegetable stuffing:

In a large sauce pan, melt 2 tablespoons butter and add the onion,
celery, mushrooms, carrots, ½ tablespoon thyme, ½ tablespoon basil,
1 tablespoon hot sauce and 1 tablespoon of Amazing Taste® Chicken
Seasoning and mix well.

Stuff the bird. If you have some stuffing leftover, place it around the pan
or cook it in the oven in a small container.

Make a paste with the 1 remaining tablespoon of hot sauce and the rest
of the Amazing Taste® Chicken Seasoning. Coat chicken with the paste
and place in a roasting pan large enough to hold the chicken. Put in
the oven uncovered and cook until the internal temperature of the meat
reaches 165°F. As always, let your meat thermometer be your guide. If
it starts browning too much use a foil tent.

Transfer cooked chicken to a cutting board. Let rest for about 5
minutes, carve and serve.

chicken kabobs

chicken breast, 1 pound, boneless & skinless
onion*, 1, medium-sized, cut into 1 inch squares
bell peppers, 3, medium-sized (choose your favorite colors)
olive oil, 2 tablespoons
Amazing Taste® Malibu Seasoning, 1 packet

additional items:
wood** or metal skewers

Thread the skewers, alternating chicken and vegetable squares. Brush chicken, onion and bell peppers with olive oil and then sprinkle with Amazing Taste® Malibu Seasoning.

Heat grill to MEDIUM-HIGH heat. Cook kabobs 6 to 8 minutes per side or until the internal temperature of the chicken reaches 165°F.

*Use veggies of your choice! The varying colors of peppers and onions can bring a different aesthetic appeal to your dish – and remember, some types of onions are sweeter than others.

**Be sure to soak wood skewers in water first or they may burn!

zesty chicken fajitas

olive oil, 2 teaspoons
chicken breast (or beef sirloin), 1 pound, boneless & skinless, trimmed, cut into thin strips about ½ inch thick
onion, 1, medium-sized
green bell pepper, 1, medium-sized, rinsed*, seeded, halved and cut lengthwise into thin strips
lime juice, ¾ cup
Amazing Taste® Fajita Seasoning, 1 packet
tomatoes, 4, small, rinsed*, halved & and cut lengthwise into thin strips
tortillas, 8, flour or corn

In a large skillet, heat olive oil on MEDIUM heat and add all ingredients (except tomatoes and tortillas), including the Amazing Taste® Fajita Seasoning. Sauté for approximately 4 minutes. Then, add tomatoes and cook for an additional 1 to 2 minutes.

Spoon into warm tortillas and serve the extra filling on the side. Don't be afraid to encourage everyone to eat with their hands. It's part of the fun!

*After rinsing the vegetables make sure to dry them thoroughly. This will keep water on the vegetables from popping in the hot oil.

spicy chicken wings

chicken wings, 2 pounds
Amazing Taste® Chicken Seasoning, 1 packet
hot sauce, ½ cup
water, ½ cup
lime juice, 1 teaspoon
olive oil, 2 tablespoons

Preheat oven to 400°F.

Rinse chicken wings in cold running water. Mix Amazing Taste® Chicken Seasoning, hot sauce, water, lime juice and olive oil in a small bowl.

Place wings in a baking dish and pour sauce over them, covering evenly. Let the wings marinate for 15 minutes or longer for extra flavor. Place wings on a baking pan.

Bake uncovered at 400°F for 30 minutes.

Serve while still warm for that tingling spicy hot experience that you expect from chicken wings.

Celery sticks with ranch or blue cheese dressing are good on the side.

italian turkey meatballs

ground turkey, 1 pound, lean
tomato sauce, ¼ cup, no salt added
parmesan cheese, 2 tablespoons, grated
oregano leaves, ¼ teaspoon
Amazing Taste® Burger Seasoning, 1 packet

Preheat oven to 350°F.

Combine all ingredients in a medium-sized bowl and mix thoroughly.
Using a tablespoon and your hands, scoop and form the mixture into
small balls that are about 1 inch in diameter. Place the meatballs on a
lightly oiled cookie sheet.

Bake at 350°F for about 25 minutes, or until the internal temperature
reaches a minimum of 165°F.

Serve with pasta. Just for surprise, pick some different shaped pastas.
You can make these a little smaller and serve as a first course or party
food.

1 hour and 15 minutes start to finish
SERVES 4

turkey meatloaf

ground turkey (or beef), 1 pound, lean
onion, 2 tablespoons, chopped
ketchup, 2 tablespoons
Worcestershire sauce, 1 teaspoon
Amazing Taste® Burger Seasoning, ½ packet

Preheat oven to 375°F.

Add all ingredients to ground turkey and mix well. Shape into a loaf in a shallow baking pan or loaf pan. Coat with additional ketchup.

Bake uncovered for 1 hour or until the internal temperature reaches 165°F.

Remove from the oven and let stand for 10 minutes before serving.

turkey & scrambled eggs

ground turkey, 1 pound, lean
Amazing Taste® Chicken Seasoning, 1 packet
eggs, 4
cheddar cheese, ½ cup, shredded
pitted black olives, 2 tablespoons, chopped
hot sauce or chili sauce, 2 tablespoons
olive oil, 2 tablespoons
parsley or chives, 1 tablespoon (optional), chopped

Combine ground turkey and the Amazing Taste® Chicken Seasoning and set it aside.

In a small bowl, beat the eggs until light and fluffy. Add cheddar cheese, olives and hot sauce to the eggs. Mix very well.

In a large skillet, heat olive oil on MEDIUM-HIGH and brown the turkey until it's no longer pink. Add the egg mixture to the browned turkey and stir until eggs are cooked.

Serve sprinkled with chopped parsley or some chopped chives, if desired. This makes a lovely dinner omelet. Serve with Sweet Potato Wedges (on page 123).

pilgrim's rice bowl

olive oil, 2 tablespoons
ground turkey, 1 pound
onion, 1 cup, chopped
celery, 1 cup, chopped
mushroom, 1 cup, sliced
Amazing Taste® Chicken Seasoning, 1 packet
rice, ½ cup, uncooked
water or chicken broth, 1 ¼ cup, low-sodium
parsley, 2 teaspoons, dried

In a medium lidded saucepan, heat the olive oil and cook the ground turkey on MEDIUM-HIGH heat for 2 to 3 minutes. Toss in onion and celery and continue cooking until the onion is translucent. Add mushroom and continue cooking until the turkey is browned. Add Amazing Taste® Chicken Seasoning, rice, water (or chicken broth) and the parsley flakes, and bring to a boil.

Reduce the heat to MEDIUM-LOW and cover. Simmer for 50 to 60 minutes, or until water is absorbed.

Fluff with a fork and serve with a sprinkle of chopped scallions or chives for a little extra go-to flavor.

festive holiday turkey

turkey, 9-12 pounds, thawed or fresh
butter, 1 cup
onion, 1 cup, chopped
celery, 1 cup, chopped
mushroom, 1 cup, sliced
herb stuffing, 6 cups
chicken broth (or water), 1 ¼ cups, low-sodium
Amazing Taste® Chicken Seasoning, 2 packets (2 ounces)
rosemary, ½ teaspoon if dry, 1 ½ teaspoons if fresh
thyme, ½ teaspoon if dry, 1 ½ teaspoons if fresh

Rinse the turkey in cold running water, pat dry and set it aside.
On MEDIUM-HIGH heat, sauté vegetables in ¼ cup of butter for 3 to 4 minutes, or until the onions are translucent. Combine the veggies with herb stuffing in a medium-sized bowl. Add the chicken broth (or water), along with ¼ cup melted butter (or olive oil) and mix well.

Coat the neck and interior of the bird with 2 tablespoons Amazing Taste® Chicken Seasoning before spooning the stuffing inside the body and neck cavities, allowing for a little bit of expansion during roasting*. The remaining stuffing should be put in a covered baking dish, to cook for the last 45 minutes.

Truss or skewer both body openings.

Melt ½ cup of butter and add the remaining Amazing Taste® Chicken Seasoning and rosemary and thyme. Mix well. Coat the outside of the turkey with the marinade.

Bake in a roasting pan at 425°F for the first 15 minutes. Then, reduce the temperature to 325°F and continue cooking until the internal temperature reaches 165°F, basting every 30 minutes. Make sure you check the temperature in the leg, breast and thigh. You may want to use a tent of aluminum foil to cover the breast during the last hour. Check for doneness with a meat thermometer. When I add the foil, I put a few water soaked toothpicks in the turkey so the foil doesn't touch the nice crispy skin.

Remove turkey from roasting pan and place on a platter or carving board. It's important to let it stand for at least 10 or 15 minutes even though it looks ready to eat and you're dying to have a bite. This allows the juices to re-disperse themselves throughout the turkey. It will be juicier and easier to carve.

Carving at the table, if you're willing, is fun as everyone gets to watch. If you don't feel you're ready for a public performance you can always do it in the kitchen. Either way, your turkey is going to give everyone a delicious holiday memory.

black bean turkey burger

ground turkey, 1 pound,
black beans, 1 can (15 ounces), reduced-sodium (drain and discard the liquid)
Amazing Taste® Chili Seasoning, 1 packet
whole wheat buns, 6 (or use french bread cut thickly)
avocado, 2, sliced, halved, pitted & sliced
salsa or pico de gallo, ¾ cup

In a large bowl, combine the meat, drained black beans and Amazing Taste® Chili Seasoning.

Form mixture into 6 patties.

Grill or cook in a pan over MEDIUM heat for 4 to 5 minutes on each side until done. Turkey should reach a minimum internal temperature of 165°F (if using beef, should reach a minimum internal temperature of 160°F.)

Slice avocados and warm buns in the microwave for a few seconds if desired.

Place each patty on a bun and cover with salsa and avocado slices.

*Don't fill all the space on your grill with food. Always keep some space available so you have room to maneuver food around as it cooks, to avoid overcooking.

notes

pork

Pork is a favorite meat in many households and it's a prized dish in many cultures. Luckily, versatile pork is a growing favorite in America. It is still relatively inexpensive and available almost everywhere.

You know how we are all talking "healthy"... well, pork is an amazing source of vitamins and minerals. No matter which recipe you choose, pork is packed with protein, zinc, phosphorous, vitamin B-6, B-12, niacin, riboflavin and thiamin. It's also, of course, full of flavor, so eat more of this stuff. And tell everybody at your table who is giving you compliments, "It's good for you!"

You can prepare pork very simply, just a little Amazing Taste® and the meat is fabulous without a lot of fussing.

You can easily dress up pork, because it blends well and compliments a variety of flavors. Some like it sweet, some like it hot, and with this range of recipes you'll discover the way you like it best.

pork & scrambled eggs

ground pork, 1 pound
Amazing Taste® Pork Seasoning, 1 packet
olive oil, 2 tablespoons
mushrooms, 1 cup, sliced
onion, 1 cup, chopped
tomato, 1 cup, chopped
hot sauce, 1 teaspoon
eggs, 4, beaten

Mix Amazing Taste® Pork Seasoning with ground pork. In a large skillet, heat olive oil on MEDIUM-HIGH and cook the meat for 2 minutes.

Add veggies and hot sauce, and cook, stirring continuously for 5 to 6 minutes or until the meat is nearly done.

Add beaten eggs and let the ingredients simmer, stirring frequently until thoroughly cooked.

Serve and enjoy. This dish is great served à la carte or between two pieces of toast or on an English muffin.

farmer's pork & rice delight

olive oil, 2 tablespoons
ground pork, 1 pound
onion, 1 cup, chopped
bell pepper, 1 cup, chopped
Amazing Taste® Pork Seasoning, 1 packet
rice, 1 cup, uncooked, white
water, 2 ½ cups
soy sauce, 1 tablespoon or to taste, low-sodium

In a medium, lidded saucepan, heat the olive oil and brown ground pork on MEDIUM-HIGH heat. When browned, toss in the onion, bell pepper and Amazing Taste® Pork Seasoning. Add rice, water and soy sauce, and bring to a boil.

Reduce the heat to MEDIUM or MEDIUM-LOW and cover. Simmer for 60 minutes or until water is absorbed.

Fluff with a fork and serve – maybe with some lemon wedges or pickled ginger on the side.

seaside pork & egg brunch

ground pork, 1 pound
Amazing Taste® Pork Seasoning, 1 tablespoon
olive oil, 2 tablespoons
eggs, 4
salsa, ½ cup
cheddar cheese, ½ cup, shredded

In a medium-sized bowl, mix the ground pork with 1 tablespoon of Amazing Taste® Pork Seasoning. Fold over package and reserve rest of seasoning for later use.

Heat olive oil on MEDIUM in a large skillet with a lid. Cook the ground pork until it's almost done.

When the pork is nearly cooked, use a spoon to separate the pork while still in the skillet into 4 portions, forming 4 small pockets for the eggs.

Crack each egg into a small saucer and pour one at a time into the holes, not breaking the yolks if possible.

Spread salsa over the top of the skillet mixture. Top with shredded cheddar cheese and cover the skillet with a lid. Cook on MEDIUM heat until the cheese is melted.

To serve, scoop from underneath the egg/pork pockets with a spatula. You want the egg to stay in place in the pork pocket. This looks great when you serve it on a platter or on individual plates. Try it with some Southwest Corn Sauté on the side (on page 125).

baked pork chops & beans

pork tenderloin chops, 2 (4-6 ounces each)
Amazing Taste® Pork Seasoning, 1 packet
olive oil, 2 tablespoons
cabbage, ½ cup, sliced
mushroom, ¼ cup, sliced
onion, ¼ cup, medium-sized, sliced
baked beans, 1 can (16 ounces)

Sprinkle Amazing Taste® Pork Seasoning on each side of the pork chops, coating very well. Keep the remaining seasoning for later use. In a large skillet, heat the oil on MEDIUM-HIGH and brown the pork chops on both sides. Don't worry about completely cooking them yet.

After browning the pork chops, add the raw vegetables and the remaining Amazing Taste® Pork Seasoning to the skillet. Mix and cook for about 5 to 6 more minutes.

Add the can of beans including the liquid to the skillet and let simmer for 10 minutes.

grilled pork chops & veggies

pork loin chops, 4, ¾ inch thick
mushrooms, 4, large
tomatoes, 2, large, cut in half
onion, 1, large, sliced
Amazing Taste® Pork Seasoning, 1 packet
white wine, ¼ cup
hot sauce, 1 teaspoon

In a large pan, place the pork chops and vegetables. Combine Amazing Taste® Pork Seasoning with white wine and hot sauce and pour over the pork chops and veggies to cover.

Preheat grill to MEDIUM-HIGH. Place the vegetables on a sheet of aluminum foil, folding it over to make a pouch and sealing the edges. Place the chops on the grill, along with the veggie pouch, and brush the remaining marinade over the chops.

Grill the chops and the vegetables 7 to 9 minutes per side, or until the internal temperature reaches 145°F. Discard the remaining marinade.

pineapple salsa pork chops

pork chops, 4, approximately ¾ inch thick
Amazing Taste® Pork Seasoning, ½ packet
olive oil, 2 tablespoons

pineapple salsa:
pineapple, 6 rings, cut in ½ inch thick slices, fresh or canned
jalapeño, 1, halved lengthwise, seeds & veins removed
cilantro, 2 tablespoons, stemmed & chopped
lime juice, 2 tablespoons

Pork chops:

Sprinkle both sides of the pork chops with Amazing Taste® Pork
Seasoning, coating evenly.

Heat grill to MEDIUM-HIGH heat and oil the surface of the grill. Grill
the pork until its internal temperature reaches a minimum of 145°F,
approximately 4 to 5 minutes per side. Remove chops from the grill and
let them rest for 5 minutes.

Pineapple salsa:

While pork chops are cooking, grill the cut pineapple and jalapeños
lightly on each side*.

Dice the pineapple and jalapeño. Combine pineapple, jalapeño, cilantro
and lime juice in a small bowl. Stir together gently, creating your salsa.
Serve your pork chops with salsa drizzled on top, or off to the side for
dipping.

*Use kitchen gloves when handling chilies. Did you know... the longer
you grill the jalapeño the milder it becomes?

iowa pork chops

pork chops, 4, ¾ – 1-inch thick
Amazing Taste® Pork Seasoning, 1 packet

sauce:
onion, ½ cup, finely chopped
brown sugar, 4 tablespoons
orange peel, 1 teaspoon
ketchup, ½ cup
soy sauce, 3 tablespoons
vinegar, 2 tablespoons
Worcestershire sauce, 2 tablespoons

Preheat oven to 350°F.

Sprinkle Amazing Taste® Pork Seasoning on both sides of pork chops, coating them well.

Place pork chops in a shallow baking dish and bake for 20 minutes.

Combine sauce ingredients in a saucepan and let them simmer for 5 minutes. Pour the mixture into a blender and purée.

Cover pork chops with the sweet sauce and continue baking for an additional 10 minutes or until the internal temperature reaches 145°F.

Remove from the oven and let the chops rest for 3 to 5 minutes before serving.

pork lettuce wraps

pork loin chops or tenderloin, 1 pound, cut into ½ inch strips
Amazing Taste® Pork Seasoning, ½ packet
olive oil, 1 tablespoon
tortillas, 4, whole wheat (or your favorite kind)
lettuce, 2 cups, shredded
cheddar cheese, 1 cup, shredded
black olives, ½ cup, sliced
pico de gallo, ½ cup (chopped tomatoes, onions and cilantro)

Cut the pork into ½ inch strips and sprinkle on ½ packet of Amazing Taste® Pork Seasoning, coating evenly.

In a large skillet, add olive oil and heat on MEDIUM. Sauté the pork for about 5 minutes or until it's cooked through.

Arrange lettuce, cheese, pico de gallo, olives and cooked pork strips in the center of each tortilla. Fold the sides of the tortillas toward the center and roll up from the "bottoms" to enclose the ingredients in a yummy pocket of deliciousness. You may omit the tortillas and simply use large lettuce leaves as a wrap.

Use toothpicks or foil to help keep the wraps together. Cut in half and serve.

bbq black-eyed peas & pork loin

pork loin, 1 pound
Amazing Taste® Pork Seasoning, 1 packet
black-eyed peas, 1 can (15 ounces)
onion, 1, chopped
green bell pepper, 1, chopped
red bell pepper, 1, chopped
bbq sauce, ½ cup

Preheat oven to 400°F.

In a baking dish, cover pork loin with ½ packet of Amazing Taste® Pork Seasoning. Surround the loin with black-eyed peas, onion and bell peppers.

Cook in the oven for 45 minutes or until the internal temperature is minimum 145°F. Add your favorite barbecue sauce during the last 15 minutes of cooking or be creative and make your own sauce with some ketchup, chili powder, a dash of hot sauce, some lemon juice and whatever else you have around that will perk up the taste.

Allow the meat to cool and serve!

pulled pork sandwich

olive oil, 2 tablespoons
pork shoulder or butt, 2 pounds, boneless & trimmed of excess
fat (ask your butcher for help with getting the right cut)
onion, 1 ½ cups, chopped
water, 2 cups
yellow mustard, 1 tablespoon
prepared horseradish, 1 tablespoon
Worcestershire sauce, 1 tablespoon
Amazing Taste® Pork Seasoning, 1 packet
whole wheat buns, 8

Heat olive oil in a large roasting pan with a lid on MEDIUM-HIGH heat. Place the pork in the pan and brown all sides for about 10 minutes, adding the onion after the first 5 minutes.

Add water, mustard, horseradish, Worcestershire sauce and Amazing Taste® Pork Seasoning to the roasting pan and mix in well. Bring the mixture to a boil.

Reduce the heat and allow the mixture to simmer for 2 hours, turning the pork occasionally while it's cooking. Check frequently and keep cooking until all moisture has evaporated and a thick sauce remains.

Remove the pork shoulder, placing it on a cutting board and shred the pork with two forks, removing any excess fat.

Return the shredded pork to the pan and mix well with the sauce. Serve on buns. It's also delicious over rice or noodles.

margarita baby back ribs

baby back ribs, 2 pounds
margarita mix, ½ cup (your favorite flavor)
Amazing Taste® Pork Seasoning, 1 packet

Preheat oven to 300°F.

Place the baby back ribs on an ovenproof platter or dish. In a bowl, combine margarita mix and Amazing Taste® Pork Seasoning. Mix the ingredients together well. Coat the ribs on all sides with the margarita marinade.

Put the tray in the oven and bake for about 1 ½ hours, until the meat slips right off the bone. Tender and soft is what we are looking for.

Serve, enjoy and don't worry about sticky fingers as a few damp napkins or wipes will keep you presentable.

1 hour start to finish
SERVES 2

chili pork ribs

pork loin back ribs, 1 ½ pounds, cut into 8 separate ribs
Amazing Taste® Chili Seasoning, 1 packet
olive oil, 2 tablespoons
onion, 1 cup, sliced
diced tomatoes, 1 can (14.5 ounces), no-salt added
water, 1 cup
red beans, 1 can (15 ounces)

Sprinkle Amazing Taste® Chili Seasoning to cover all the ribs.

Heat the olive oil on MEDIUM-HIGH in a large pot and brown the ribs on all sides for 5 to 7 minutes.

Add the onion, tomato, water and the remaining Amazing Taste® Chili Seasoning to the pot and bring it to a boil. Reduce the heat to simmer for 30 minutes.

Add the beans, including the liquid, and continue simmering for at least 15 minutes, or until the meat is fork tender.

Serve and don't worry about getting messy. These ribs are finger licking good.

notes

seafood

Fish lovers enjoy their fish fresh, but not all of us have access to just-caught fish. With new freeze-right-on-the-ship techniques some frozen fish is actually even fresher. Look for individually packaged frozen fish and seafood. You'll find it's a great alternative and very convenient to store in the freezer. It's nice to always have a healthy meal at hand.

Fish used to be called "brain food"; don't laugh. Nutritionists are finding out that fish really does have special vitamins and oils that can go straight to the brain (and the rest of our body, of course).

Fish shouldn't be over-cooked so if you are looking for a meal you can turn around in a snap, fish or seafood is a great choice.

I'm happy eating fresh fish with a little olive oil or butter and a squeeze of lemon. But we have to be more adventurous than that as the recipes in this section will show. Pay more attention than usual to cooking times and test the texture as you go. A small quantity of shrimp can go a long way to create an impressive meal. Scallops have a nutty kind of taste that's worth exploring. My guests don't notice, but when I have to do some fast but satisfying entertaining, I get cooked shrimp from the seafood counter and add a couple of sauces on the side. I have an instant party that doesn't take time and toil.

If you know your guests like clams, oysters or mussels, I can promise you they will be dazzled if you add some - with or without shells - as you are finishing your pasta sauce.

Don't believe the strict foodies who say to only drink white wine with fish. I find that soft drinks, red wine, or beer do just fine. It's your creation from the sea that counts.

baked catfish & veggies

catfish fillets, 1 pound (4 fillets)
Amazing Taste® Seafood Seasoning, 1 packet
white wine, ¼ cup
olive oil, ¼ cup
lemon juice, ¼ cup
bell pepper, 1 cup, chopped
onion, 1 cup, chopped
tomato, 1 cup, chopped
mushroom, 1 cup, chopped

Preheat oven to 425°F.

Place catfish in a large baking dish. In a small bowl, combine Amazing Taste® Seafood Seasoning with all the liquid ingredients. Pour sauce over the catfish, coating well.

Add the chopped vegetables to the dish, making sure they get coated well with the sauce.

Bake for 25 minutes or until the fish fillets are flaky to the touch and the vegetables are tender. Be careful not to overcook.

spicy cajun catfish

marinade:
hot sauce, 2 tablespoons
Amazing Taste® Malibu Seasoning, 1 tablespoon
olive oil, 4 tablespoons

fish:
catfish, 1 pound, cut into 1" x 3" strips
corn meal, ½ cup

In a large bowl combine hot sauce, Amazing Taste® Malibu Seasoning and 2 tablespoons of olive oil in a bowl. Stir together.

Dip strips of the catfish in the marinade and then coat evenly with corn meal on each side.

Heat remaining 2 tablespoons of olive oil in a large frying pan on MEDIUM-HIGH.

Fry the fish for about 3 minutes on each side or until done.

35 minutes start to finish
SERVES 4

lemon dill salmon

salmon fillets, 4 (4 ounces each)
broccoli & cauliflower floret mixture, 4 cups, fresh
olive oil, ½ cup
lemon juice, ½ cup
Amazing Taste® Seafood Seasoning, 1 packet
dill, as a garnish (optional)

Preheat oven to 375°F.

Place the salmon in a shallow baking pan and surround it with vegetables.

In a small bowl, combine olive oil, lemon juice and Amazing Taste® Seafood Seasoning, mixing well into a delicious marinade.

Thoroughly coat all surfaces of fillets and vegetables with the marinade. Cover and bake for 30 minutes – or until fish are flaky at the touch of a fork – with a minimum internal temperature of 145°F.

Scissor some fresh dill on top when you serve, if desired.

tangy cod curry

curry powder, 4 tablespoons
Amazing Taste® Malibu Seasoning, 2 tablespoons
lemon juice, ½ cup
olive oil, ½ cup
cod fillets, 4 (6 ounces each)
tomatoes, 2, large-sized, quartered
mushrooms, 1 cup, quartered
onions, 1 cup, sliced
jalapeños*, 2, sliced, deveined & seeded

Preheat oven to 400°F.

In a small bowl mix curry powder, Amazing Taste® Malibu Seasoning, lemon juice and olive oil. Stir until you have a kind of paste.

Arrange cod fillets, tomatoes, mushrooms, onions and jalapeños in a baking dish, and pour the sauce mixture on top of them. If not everyone likes it hot, you may want to cook the jalapeños separately and add them only for those who're ready for extra spicy.

Bake at 400°F covered for 20 to 30 minutes (or until the cod's internal temperature reaches 145°F) and the fish flakes at the touch of a fork.

*Wear kitchen gloves when handling the jalapeños.

tilapia chili

olive oil, 2 tablespoons
tilapia, 1 pound, chopped into bite-sized pieces
onion, 1 cup, chopped
water, ½ cup
tomato, 1 can (14.5 ounces), diced, no salt added
kidney beans, 1 can (15.5 ounces), drained
Amazing Taste® Chili Seasoning, 1 packet

In a large, lidded pot, heat oil on MEDIUM-HIGH.

Add the tilapia and chopped onion and brown for 5 minutes, being careful not to overcook. Tilapia is thin so check regularly.

Add water, tomatoes, kidney beans and Amazing Taste® Chili seasoning. Mix very well and bring to a boil.

Cover and reduce heat, allowing the ingredients to cook for 10 minutes. Stir occasionally.

Serve with shredded cheddar cheese, salsa and chopped cilantro, if desired.

malibu fish tacos

fish fillets*, 4 (4 ounces each)
Amazing Taste® Malibu Seasoning, 1 packet
olive oil, 1 tablespoon
tortillas, 8, corn or flour, warmed on an open burner
lettuce or cabbage, 1 cup, finely shredded
chunky salsa or pico de gallo, 1 cup
sour cream, ½ cup
avocado, 1, large, ripe, halved, pitted & sliced (squeeze lemon or lime juice to maintain color)

Sprinkle each side of the fish with Amazing Taste® Malibu Seasoning.

In a large skillet, heat olive oil on MEDIUM. Place seasoned fish in the pan and cook 2 ½ minutes per side or until done.

Cut fish fillets in half. Layer fish and shredded lettuce or cabbage into the warmed tortillas and serve with salsa, sour cream and avocado on the side. I like to flavor the sour cream with lemon or lime juice.

*Tilapia or any light, white fish is recommended.

salmon fajitas

salmon fillet, 1 pound, cut into ½ strips
lime, 1
Amazing Taste® Fajita Seasoning, 1 tablespoon
olive oil, 2 tablespoons
green bell pepper, 1, sliced
red bell pepper, 1, sliced
onion, 1, sliced
cilantro, ¼ cup, chopped
tortillas, 8, corn or flour, warmed on an open burner

Squeeze lime juice on the salmon. Coat all surfaces of the salmon with Amazing Taste® Fajita Seasoning.

In a large skillet, heat olive oil on MEDIUM and place salmon in skillet, arranging vegetables around the fish. Cook for 5 minutes, stirring occasionally and adding cilantro about 30 seconds before you finish cooking.

Serve with tortillas, salsa or flavored mayo and avocados on the side.

25 minutes start to finish
SERVES 4

tomato garlic shrimp pizza

pizza crust*, 12-inch, thin
pizza sauce, ½ cup
raw shrimp, 1 pound, peeled & deveined
Amazing Taste® Seafood Seasoning, 1 packet
mushrooms, ½ cup, sliced
tomato, ½ cup, chopped
green onion, ½ cup, chopped
garlic, 2 teaspoons, minced
parsley, 2 tablespoons
olive oil, 3 tablespoons
lemon juice, 1 tablespoon

Preheat the oven to 425°F. Spread the pizza sauce on the pizza crust.

In a large bowl, place the shrimp and coat with Amazing Taste® Seafood Seasoning. Add all other ingredients and mix well.

Spread this mixture on the pizza crust, covering it as evenly as you can, and bake on a greased cookie sheet until crust is crispy and the shrimp is cooked. This should take around 15 minutes. Grate some fresh parmesan or mozzarella cheese on top of the pizza during the last 5 minutes of cooking time, if desired, or on the side.

Remove from the oven and let it stand for 5 minutes. Slice into 8 pieces and serve.

*There are a lot of choices. Ready-made pizza crusts are available fresh, refrigerated or frozen. You can also purchase frozen or refrigerated pizza dough that you knead and roll out yourself.

shrimp lettuce wraps

olive oil, 2 tablespoons
hot sauce, 2 teaspoons
soy sauce, 6 tablespoons, reduced-sodium
white wine, ½ cup
Amazing Taste® Seafood Seasoning, 1 packet
raw shrimp, 1 pound, peeled & deveined
red cabbage, 2 cups, chopped or shredded
carrot, 2 cups
water chestnuts, ½ cup, chopped
iceberg lettuce, 1 head (enough to pull at least 8 decent-sized leaves)

Heat a pan over MEDIUM heat. Add olive oil, hot sauce, soy sauce, white wine and Amazing Taste® Seafood Seasoning to the pan. Stir.

After about a minute, add shrimp, cabbage, carrots and water chestnuts to the pan.

Continue to cook over MEDIUM heat, stirring frequently until the vegetables are tender and the shrimp is pink.

Spoon the cooked shrimp and veggie mixture into the lettuce leaves. Roll the leaves while folding the ends toward the center. Enjoy!

You can also serve the shrimp in a bowl and the lettuce leaves on a platter and let guests build their own.

Have some light soy sauce or wedges of lemon or lime on the side.

shrimp scampi

olive oil, ¾ cup
shallots, 1 tablespoon, chopped
garlic, 2 tablespoons, minced
Amazing Taste® Seafood Seasoning, 1 packet
white wine, ½ cup
lemon juice, ¼ cup
raw shrimp, 1 ½ pounds, peeled & deveined
parsley, 2 tablespoons, chopped
tomato, 1, medium-sized, diced

Heat olive oil in a large skillet over MEDIUM heat.

Add shallots, garlic, and packet of Amazing Taste® Seafood Seasoning and stir. Add white wine, lemon juice and shrimp, and continue cooking until the shrimp turn light orange and are no longer translucent.

Toss in parsley and tomato and serve. (This dish also would be great served over Mediterranean Rice, which can be found on page 129.)

10 minutes start to finish
SERVES 4

malibu shrimp skewers

large shrimp, 1 pound, peeled & deveined
olive oil, 1 tablespoon
Amazing Taste® Malibu Seasoning, 1 packet

additional items:
wood* or metal skewers

Thread shrimp on skewers and baste with olive oil. Sprinkle the
skewers with Amazing Taste® Malibu Seasoning.

Heat grill on MEDIUM-HIGH heat. Cook shrimp skewers for 3 to 4
minutes per side or until the shrimp turns pink and are slightly charred.

For added flavor, you could also skewer mushrooms, tomatoes, bell
peppers or onions with the shrimp.

* If you use wood skewers, be sure to soak them in water for at least 10
minutes before cooking so they don't burn!

notes

sides

Think of "sides" like accessories. Side dishes are the neck tie, the pin, the boots of the meal.

The main course is central. It anchors the meal. Then the choice of food "accessories" that you serve on the side shake up the whole presentation.

When you are thinking of sides, try to pick things you feel will go together. Sometimes it adds special burst of flavor when you serve some unexpected pairings. Go past the tried and true.

Remember: cranberry sauce is not only for Turkey Day.

Some vegetables and other sides may be served cold or at room temperature, so you won't have to fuss with them as you finish the rest of your meal.

Sides can be purchased and then "home-improved." For instance, prepared cole slaw or potato salad can be dressed up with some chopped (or scissored) fresh parsley and a bit of your favorite Amazing Taste® Seasonings. "Home cooked" doesn't have to mean every single thing on the table!

Hot fruit, as well as vegetables, can be an unexpected addition. Try a little Amazing Taste® on warm fruit for a spicy flavor.

You can make some ordinary things look impressive. A tomato can look very fancy if you take a second to arrange the slices.

Side dishes complete the picture and can fill out a meal. Have some fun with these budget-friendly ideas!

zesty veggie stir fry

carrots, 2, cut into thin strips 1/8 inch by 1/8 inch by 2 inches
(Julienne*)
red bell pepper, 1 cup sliced into thin strips
yellow squash, 1 cup, chopped into ¼ inch slices
whole snow peas, 1 cup
garlic powder, 2 teaspoons (or use fresh grated garlic)
hot sauce, 1 tablespoon
soy sauce, 1 tablespoon
Amazing Taste® Malibu Seasoning, 1 tablespoon
olive oil, 2 tablespoons
green onion, ½ cup chopped

Place all vegetables in a large bowl (except the green onions) and mix. Add garlic powder, hot sauce, soy sauce and Amazing Taste® Malibu Seasoning.

Heat olive oil in a wok pan or large skillet on MEDIUM-HIGH until very hot, but not smoking. Toss in the vegetable mixture and cook for about 2 minutes, tossing continuously.

Add the green onion and cook for a minute more before serving. You don't want the vegetables to wilt. Aim for crunchy.

*Julienne: A French term for a culinary knife cut in which the food item is cut into long thin strips.

brown sugar baked carrots

carrots*, ½ pound
olive oil, 1 tablespoon
lemon juice, ½ tablespoon
brown sugar, 1 tablespoon
parsley, 1 tablespoon, chopped
Amazing Taste® Malibu Seasoning, ½ tablespoon

Preheat oven to 400°F.

Peel and cut carrots into quarters or circular slices and lay them out evenly in a baking dish.

In a small bowl, combine olive oil, lemon juice, brown sugar, parsley and Amazing Taste® Malibu Seasoning, and mix thoroughly. Maple syrup can be used in place of the brown sugar.

Pour the mixture over the carrots and cover. Bake for 30 minutes.

Everyone will love this dish... don't tell them how easy it is to prepare!

*Save time and pick up a bag of washed, ready-to-serve carrots in your grocer's produce department! You can use little carrots or pre-sliced ones.

sweet potato wedges

sweet potatoes or yams, 2 (1 pound), medium-large
canola oil, 1 tablespoon
Amazing Taste® Malibu Seasoning (to taste)
parsley, 2 tablespoons, minced

Preheat oven to 400°F. Place a baking sheet on the center rack in the oven while it's preheating.

Peel sweet potatoes and cut them in half. Then, slice each half lengthwise and cut them into wedges approximately ½ inch thick.

Place the wedges in a bowl and add the canola oil. Mix well.

Using oven mitts, remove the baking sheet from the oven. Place the potato wedges on the baking sheet and slide the baking sheet back onto the center rack. Bake at 400°F for about 10 minutes. You want them to be brown and tender. It's okay to taste one for doneness, but be careful you don't burn yourself!

Remove the baking sheet from oven and turn the wedges over (tongs are great for this).

Bake at 400°F for an additional 10 minutes or until you reach desired doneness. Again, taking one out for a little taste test is fine.

Place cooked wedges on a serving platter and season them with Amazing Taste® Malibu Seasoning. Sprinkle with parsley, toss and serve.

Hope you made plenty, because they'll go fast. These go well with our Amazing Steaks (on page 56).

10 minutes start to finish
SERVES 4

zucchini sauté

olive oil, 2 tablespoons
green zucchini, ½ pound, sliced & diced
yellow squash, ½ pound, sliced & diced
onion, ½ cup, diced
garlic powder, 1 tablespoon
Amazing Taste® Malibu Seasoning, 1 tablespoon
basil leaves, ½ tablespoon (keep some frozen basil on hand - it defrosts in seconds)

Warm oil on MEDIUM heat in a heavy frying pan. Add the zucchini and yellow squash, onion, garlic powder and Amazing Taste® Malibu Seasoning.

Cook for 5 minutes, stirring constantly. Near the end of cooking, sprinkle basil over the zucchini.

Serve in a warmed serving dish.

Mix well and you're ready to serve a yummy and very healthy dish.

southwest corn sauté

water, ½ cup, boiled
corn, ½ pound, frozen
olive oil, 1 tablespoon
onion, 1 (½ cup), diced
green bell pepper, 1 (½ cup), diced
Amazing Taste® Malibu Seasoning, ½ tablespoon
tomatoes, 2, medium-sized, diced
cilantro, ½ cup, chopped

Put water in a large skillet and cook corn for about 2 minutes, stirring to thaw.

Add olive oil, onion, green bell peppers and Amazing Taste® Malibu Seasoning to skillet with corn and sauté, stirring to combine. Add tomatoes to the mixture and sauté for another 2 to 3 minutes.

Sprinkle with chopped cilantro and serve!

easy ratatouille

olive oil, ½ cup
zucchini, 2, cut into ½ inch slices
eggplant, 1, cut into ½ inch cubes
onion, ½ cup, chopped
green bell pepper, 1, cut into strips
garlic cloves, 2, minced
Amazing Taste® Malibu Seasoning, 1 packet
tomatoes, 3, fresh, cut into wedges
tomato sauce or juice, ½ cup (optional)

Preheat the oven to 350°F.

Coat a baking dish with 1 tablespoon of olive oil. Layer the zucchini, eggplant, onion and bell pepper in the bottom of the baking dish, and cover with the remaining olive oil and minced garlic cloves. Sprinkle 2 tablespoons of Amazing Taste® Malibu Seasoning to cover.

Bake in the oven for approximately 30 minutes or until the eggplant is soft. Then, top the heated mixture with the tomato wedges and sprinkle with the remaining Amazing Taste® Malibu Seasoning. Drizzle the top with a little tomato sauce or tomato juice, if desired.

Bake for 15 additional minutes and remove from the oven. Let stand covered for 3 minutes before serving.

sautéed mushrooms

olive oil, 2 tablespoons

mushrooms, 1 pound, sliced (I prefer baby bella, but any white mushrooms will work)

Amazing Taste® Malibu Seasoning, 2 teaspoons

garlic powder, 2 teaspoons

white wine, ½ cup

green onions, ¼ cup, chopped (you can also use 2 tablespoons of chopped chives or shallots)

Heat the olive oil in a pan on MEDIUM heat. Add all ingredients (except green onions) and sauté for about 5 minutes.

Add the green onions and continue to sauté for another 30 seconds. It's that fast to create a terrific compliment to your main course!

Now you're ready to serve.

50 minutes start to finish
SERVES 4

mushroom rice pilaf

olive oil, 2 tablespoons
chicken broth, 1 can (14 ounces), no salt added
water, ¾ cup
onion, 1 cup, chopped
mushrooms, 1 cup, thinly sliced
whole grain brown rice, 1 cup
Amazing Taste® Malibu Seasoning, 1 tablespoon

In a medium, lidded saucepan, heat olive oil on MEDIUM-HIGH. Meanwhile, in a small saucepan, bring the broth and water to a boil.

When the oil is hot but not smoking, sauté the onions and mushrooms until the onion is slightly translucent (for about 2 to 3 minutes).

Add the uncooked rice to the saucepan and sauté, stirring constantly for about a minute or until the rice is fully coated with olive oil.

Add the hot broth, water and Amazing Taste® Malibu Seasoning and stir. Bring to a boil.

Reduce the heat to LOW and cover. Simmer for 45 minutes, or until water is absorbed.

If you have shelled pine nuts you can add those for a different touch. You can also add dry currants.

Fluff with a fork and serve!

mediterranean rice

olive oil, 2 tablespoons
onion, ½ cup, shredded
carrot, ½ cup, chopped
bell pepper, ½ cup, chopped
mushrooms, ½ cup, chopped
jasmine rice, 1 cup (rinsed according to package instructions)
chicken broth, 1 can (14 ounces), low-sodium
Amazing Taste® Malibu Seasoning, 1 tablespoon

In a large skillet with a lid, heat olive oil on MEDIUM-HIGH. Sauté the onion, carrots, bell pepper, and mushrooms for 4 to 5 minutes.

Add rice, chicken broth and Amazing Taste® Malibu Seasoning, and mix everything together very well.

Bring to a boil. Cover, reduce the heat to LOW, and simmer for 45 minutes or until the water has evaporated. When all liquid is absorbed, the rice is ready. Be careful not to let the rice dry out or burn.

Fluff with a fork and serve!

microwave magic

The microwave is hot-hot-hot!! I'm not talking about suggested temperature. The often poorly regarded and under appreciated microwave oven has been re-discovered. What was once thought of as a good place to heat leftovers or refresh a cup of coffee, has now reached gourmet status. Many fine restaurants don't want you to know that their kitchens include microwave ovens to perform tasks that previously took a long time to prepare; no one would suspect have been cooked in their secret microwave.

Throw out your old ideas about microwave cooking and give that crafty little box a second chance.

Don't ever think that a microwave is only good for boiling water or popping corn! Perhaps one of the most revolutionary kitchen devices of modern cooking has been the microwave oven. More and more people are finding out that microwaving is a more convenient way to cook. You can discover how to reduce defrosting and cooking times to nearly nothing. Certain foods (try meat and poultry) taste spectacular when cooked in the microwave. Try some of the recipes in this book and you be the judge! Dare to cook something in the microwave you've never tried to do before. Keep notes for yourself about what works best.

At first, follow the directions in our recipes very closely so you can prove to yourself that I'm right. I'm telling you that new techniques and Amazing Taste® Seasonings (designed to optimize microwave cooking) can create great meals from the once lowly-regarded microwave. As you realize what you can do, you'll come up with new uses for speedy and yummy cooking. Please share some of your recipes with me at amazing@amazingtaste.com. I am a huge advocate and fan of the microwave so you can help me spread the word.

Fish fresh from your microwave! Don't you dare judge until you taste some of the recipes in this book. The microwave is an excellent little gadget that can cook some spectacularly fresh meals if you know how to use it properly – and if you know what's best to cook in it!

For example, seafood has numerous health benefits but many people aren't sure how to properly prepare seafood dishes. The microwave oven is the perfect way to prepare this! Fish is very high in water content and it is ideal for fast, convenient cooking in the microwave. All you need to do is season it properly and watch the settings and the timing.

Vegetables are not only an essential part of most meals, they're one of the best parts. What most people don't know is that they're also ideal for microwave cooking.

25 minutes start to finish
SERVES 4 to 6

veggie garden medley

broccoli, 1 ½ pounds
cauliflower, ½ head
zucchini, 2, sliced
tomatoes, 2, cut into wedges
olive oil, 3 tablespoons
Amazing Taste® Malibu Seasoning, 2 teaspoons
garlic powder, ½ teaspoon
parmesan cheese, ½ cup, grated

Trim the broccoli, cutting it into pieces about 2 ½ inches long with stalks about ¼ inch thick. On a microwave-safe serving platter, arrange the broccoli with the florets pointed toward the outer edge.

Cut cauliflower into similar-sized florets. Place a row of them around the platter, just on the inside of the broccoli.

Do the same with the zucchini, placing it just on the inside of the cauliflower ring, and then mound the tomatoes in the center.

Microwave, covered, on HIGH for 12 minutes, and then let stand with the cover still in place for another 5 minutes.

In a small bowl, pour in olive oil and Amazing Taste® Malibu Seasoning. Microwave the mixture on HIGH for 1 minute.

Drizzle the olive oil mixture over your vegetables and sprinkle with garlic powder and parmesan cheese.

Serve with a meal or as an appetizer with toothpicks.

broccoli & cheese casserole

broccoli, 1 ½ cups, chopped
celery, 1 cup, chopped
mushroom, 1 cup, sliced
onion, ½ cup, chopped
water, 2 tablespoons
Amazing Taste® Malibu Seasoning, 1 tablespoon
condensed cream of mushroom soup, 1 can (10 ¾ ounces)
parmesan cheese, 1 cup, grated

In a microwave-safe dish, place broccoli, celery, mushroom, onion, water and Amazing Taste® Malibu Seasoning. Mix well, then cover and microwave on HIGH for 5 minutes.

Stir and mix in soup and cheese to the cooked vegetables. Microwave, covered, on HIGH for 5 more minutes. Stir well.

Let stand, covered, for 5 minutes before serving.

10 minutes start to finish
SERVES 4

asparagus with hollandaise sauce

asparagus, ¾ pound (1 fresh bunch)
water, ¼ cup

hollandaise sauce (makes ¾ cup):
butter, ½ cup
fresh lemon juice, 1 tablespoon
Amazing Taste® Malibu Seasoning, 2 teaspoons
egg yolks, 3, beaten

Cut about ½ inch off the ends of the asparagus stalks.

In a microwave safe dish, place asparagus with tips pointing toward the center. Add water and cover.

Microwave on HIGH for 6 minutes or until tender. A little less cooking time will add some crunch. Just be careful not to overcook.

Let the asparagus stand, covered, while you prepare the hollandaise sauce.

Hollandaise is a delicate sauce and it may take a couple of tries to get it right but it's worth the effort.

Put the butter, lemon juice and Amazing Taste® Malibu Seasoning into a small microwave-safe bowl. Microwave on HIGH for 2 minutes, or until the ingredients are bubbly. Stir.

Slowly add in the melted butter mixture to the beaten egg yolks, beating constantly with a whisk. Serve immediately. Warning - do not return to the microwave to reheat! It just doesn't work.

sweet baked beans

baked beans, 2 cans (16 ounces)
onion, ½ cup, chopped
brown sugar, ¼ cup
maple syrup, 2 tablespoons
ketchup, 2 tablespoon
mustard, 1 teaspoon
Worcestershire sauce, 1 dash
Amazing Taste® Pork Seasoning, 1 tablespoon

In a microwave-safe bowl, mix all the ingredients together. Mix well, but be careful not to squish the beans.

Cover the bowl and microwave on HIGH for 12 minutes. Let the beans stand covered for about 3 minutes before serving. Offer crumbled bacon, shredded cheese and chopped onions on the side. You can substitute molasses for the maple syrup if you'd like.

10 minutes start to finish
SERVES 4

green beans almondine

almonds, ½ cup, sliced
butter, 6 tablespoons
french cut green beans, 1 frozen package (16 ounces)
garlic powder, 1 teaspoon
Amazing Taste® Malibu Seasoning, 1 tablespoon

In a small microwave-safe bowl, place almonds and 2 tablespoons of the butter. Microwave on HIGH for 3 to 4 minutes, stirring after each minute.

Place green beans in a microwave-safe serving bowl and microwave, covered, on HIGH for 5 minutes. Let stand.

In another small bowl, place 4 tablespoons of butter, garlic powder and Amazing Taste® Malibu Seasoning. Microwave on HIGH for 30 seconds, or until butter is melted.

Drain any excess liquid from the green beans and toss them together with the almond slivers. (You can lightly toast them if you like for a little extra crunch.) Drizzle with the melted butter mixture and stir well before serving.

peas & pearl onions

frozen peas, 1 package (10 ounces)
frozen small onions, 1 cup, whole
olive oil, 4 tablespoons
Amazing Taste® Malibu Seasoning, 1 tablespoon
garlic powder, 1 teaspoon
parmesan cheese, 2 tablespoons, grated

In a microwave-safe bowl, combine the frozen peas and onions. Cover and microwave on HIGH for 7 minutes. In another small bowl, pour in olive oil and Amazing Taste® Malibu Seasoning and microwave on HIGH for 30 seconds.

Drain any excess liquid from cooked vegetables. Stir well. Drizzle with olive oil, and sprinkle with garlic powder and cheese. Stir well.

wine-marinated vegetable medley

green bell pepper, 1, diced
mushroom, ½ pound, sliced
onion, ½ cup, chopped
red wine or white wine, ½ cup (or you can substitute apple juice
mixed with water)
Amazing Taste® Malibu Seasoning, 2 tablespoons
parsley, 4 tablespoons, chopped

In a microwave-safe bowl, combine all ingredients, except the parsley,
and stir well. Microwave, covered, on HIGH for 8 minutes, stirring
halfway through the cooking time. Mix in the parsley.

If you don't want to use wine, experiment with balsamic vinegar which is
also sweet and tart.

Let stand covered for 3 minutes before serving.

salisbury steak

ground beef, 1 pound
flour, 1 tablespoon
water, ¼ cup
Amazing Taste® Burger Seasoning, 1 packet
onion, ¼ cup, chopped
mushrooms, ½ cup, sliced

Shape ground beef into 4 patties. Some like to make the patties more oval than round so they look like steaks.

In a small bowl, whisk flour, water and ½ teaspoon Amazing Taste® Burger Seasoning until smooth. Save the remaining seasoning to use later in recipe.

In a shallow microwave-safe dish, combine the chopped onions and water mixture.

Microwave, covered, for 1 minute. Add sliced mushrooms and microwave again, covered, on HIGH for 1 minute. Stir well.

Sprinkle each side generously with Amazing Taste® Burger Seasoning. Arrange steaks on gravy mixture. Cover and microwave on HIGH for 7 to 9 minutes or until desired degree of doneness is reached.

Let stand, covered for 3 minutes. Spoon gravy over steaks and serve.

30 minutes start to finish
SERVES 2-4

cornish game hen

rosemary leaves, 2 teaspoons, fresh (or ½ teaspoon dried)
dry white wine, ½ cup
cornish game hens, 2, halved
Amazing Taste® Chicken Seasoning, 1 packet

In a small bowl, soak the rosemary leaves in the white wine for 10 to 15 minutes.

Arrange the hens cut side down in a 2-quart oblong baking dish. Sprinkle them lightly with white wine and rosemary mixture, then, heavily with Amazing Taste® Chicken Seasoning. The birds should be completely covered.

Pour wine/rosemary mixture around the hens, but not on them, and microwave on HIGH with the dish covered for 10 minutes.

Take dish out of the microwave and rearrange the hens, moving the center portion of the hens to the outside of the dish. Put back in the microwave again, covered, cook on HIGH for 8 to 10 minutes or until the internal temperature reaches a minimum of 165°F at the thickest part of the hen.

Let the dish stand for 5 minutes before serving.

quick corn-on-the-cob

corn on the cob, 4, fresh & husked (you can also use frozen, but adjust the time)
butter, ¼ cup
Amazing Taste® Malibu Seasoning, 1 tablespoon
water, beer, or chicken broth, ½ cup

Corn on the cob with a big difference.

In a microwavable dish with a lid, melt butter on HIGH for one minute.

Add Amazing Taste® Malibu Seasoning and the water/beer/chicken broth of your choice. Stir to dissolve. Roll the four cobs in the dish to coat well.

Cover and cook on HIGH for 10 minutes, turning the cobs over halfway through the cooking time.

Wait 2 to 3 minutes before serving.

20 minutes start to finish
SERVES 4

gourmet turkey burger

ground turkey, 1 pound, lean
Amazing Taste® Burger Seasoning, 1 packet
onion, 1, thinly sliced
tomato, 1, sliced
mushrooms, 10, sliced
green bell pepper, 1, deveined & sliced
whole wheat buns, 4

It's hard to believe, but you'll love them. Delicious burgers that taste
great and look yummy!

Shape the ground turkey into four patties and moisten both sides of
each patty with water. Sprinkle each side liberally with Amazing Taste®
Burger Seasoning.

In a microwave-safe dish, place four slices of onion and top them with
four slices of tomato and place the patties on top of slices of tomato.
Layer the mushrooms slices and a ring of green peppers on top of each
turkey patty.

Coarsely chop remaining vegetables and place them around the patties.
Sprinkle Amazing Taste® Burger Seasoning over the vegetables.

Cover and microwave on HIGH for 9 to 11 minutes or until meat reaches
desired degree of doneness. The minimum internal temperature should
be 165°F.

Let the patties stand, covered, for 3 minutes before serving them on
buns.

cooking time varies depending on size of breast
SERVES 6 to 8

golden turkey & cranberry sauce

cranberries, 1 pound
sugar, 1 ½ cups
water, ¼ cup
orange marmalade, ½ cup
turkey breast, 3-4 pounds
Amazing Taste® Chicken Seasoning, 1 packet

Why not make your own cranberry sauce? You'll end up loving it.

Cranberry sauce:

In a large mixing bowl, combine cranberries, sugar and water.
Microwave on HIGH for 6 minutes. Stir well. Add orange marmalade
and microwave on HIGH for another 2 minutes. Stir.

Pour into mold or a serving bowl. Refrigerate before serving.

Turkey breast:

Moisten all sides of the breast with water. Sprinkle ½ packet
Amazing Taste® Chicken Seasoning, making sure to coat on all sides.
Remember, Amazing Taste® not only adds flavor, it seals in the juices as
well.

In a 2-quart baking dish, place turkey breast side down. Calculate your
turkey's total cooking time by using 8 minutes per pound. Microwave
covered on HIGH for one half of the total cooking time.

After microwaving for half the cooking time, turn the breast side up.
Sprinkle with Amazing Taste® Chicken Seasoning and baste the turkey
with its own drippings.

Microwave, covered, for the second half of calculated cooking time or
until the minimum internal temperature of 165°F is reached. Baste with
drippings again.

Let stand, tented with foil, 5 to 10 minutes before carving. Serve with
that delicious homemade cranberry sauce.

asian cod

cod fillets, 2 (8-10 ounces)
green beans, ½ cup, halved & trimmed
carrots, 2, cut in half lengthwise
white onion, ½ medium-sized, cut into slices
olive oil, 2 tablespoons
soy sauce, 4 tablespoons, low-sodium
hot sauce, 1 tablespoon
Amazing Taste® Malibu Seasoning, 1 tablespoon

Rinse the cod in cold running water.

Place the fish fillets in a microwave-safe dish. Arrange the vegetables, without crowding them, around the fillets.

Pour olive oil on top of the fish and veggie medley. Then, in a small bowl, mix the soy sauce, hot sauce and Amazing Taste® Malibu Seasoning and spoon the mixture across the fish and the vegetables, making sure everything is coated evenly on all sides.

Cover the dish with a lid and microwave on HIGH for 5 to 6 minutes. When cooled, the fish should flake easily at the touch of a fork.

Let the cod sit for 1 to 2 minutes in the covered dish before serving. Try with a side dish of white or brown rice, or our Mushroom Rice Pilaf (on page 128).

20 minutes start to finish
SERVES 4

salmon with spinach & mushrooms

marinade:
Amazing Taste® Seafood Seasoning, 1 packet
lemon juice, ¼ cup
dry white wine, ¼ cup
olive oil, ¼ cup
water, ¼ cup

fish:
salmon fillets, 4 (5-7 ounces each), boneless & skinless
spinach, frozen & thawed (10 ounces), or fresh (1 ½ pounds)
mushroom, 1 cup, chopped
parmesan cheese, 1 tablespoon

In a large, covered, microwave-safe baking dish, make the marinade by adding Amazing Taste® Seafood Seasoning to all other liquid ingredients. Stir well.

Place the four fillets in the marinade with the thickest part near the outer edges of the baking dish. Cover the fish with the marinade mixture using a large spoon.

Fill all empty spaces in the baking dish with vegetables, making sure they are covered in marinade as well. Sprinkle the parmesan cheese over the fish and vegetables and cover.

Microwave on HIGH for 10 minutes, or until the fish flakes easily at the touch of a fork. This dish can also be prepared in the oven at 350°F for 20 to 30 minutes, or until the fish is flaky.

Let stand for 3 to 5 minutes before serving.

white bean halibut

halibut fillets, 2 (8-10 ounces), boneless & skinless
tomato, 1 cup, chopped
baby bella mushrooms, 1 cup, halved
green onions, ½ cup, chopped
white beans, ½ cup, canned & drained
olive oil, 1 tablespoon
Amazing Taste® Malibu Seasoning, 1 packet

Rinse the fillets in cold, running water and place them in a microwave-safe dish with the vegetables and beans scattered around the fish.

Pour olive oil onto the fish, veggies, and beans, and sprinkle Amazing Taste® Malibu Seasoning over everything. Mix the vegetables gently, making sure that the seasoning coats the fish and veggies evenly.

Cover the dish and cook on HIGH in the microwave for 5 to 6 minutes. The fish should flake apart at the touch of your fork when it's ready. Let the dish sit on the counter for about 2 minutes before serving.

cooking methods

There are two types of cooking: conventional and microwave. Conventional cooking is divided into two types as well: dry-heat cooking and moist-heat cooking.

DRY-HEAT COOKING

BROILING: cooking by application of direct radiant heat from above the food.

GRILLING: similar to broiling, except the heat source comes from below the food.

Because air is a poor conductor of heat, broiling and grilling require the food to be in close proximity to the heat source.

BARBEQUING: similar to grilling, except it is done slowly with low-cooking temperatures and a lot of smoke.

From what I've learned from my dad and experimenting with food personally, the correct way to barbeque is whatever works for you. The only way to get really good at barbecuing is to practice.

Broiling, grilling and barbecuing are great ways to cook tender cuts of beef, chicken, fish and vegetables. Grilling is considered a healthy way of cooking because much of the fat will drip out during the cooking process.

CONVECTION: the definition of convection cooking is "circulating air." In a convection oven, a fan circulates hot air over, under and around the food. As a result, foods are evenly cooked and browned, often in a shorter cooking time and at a lower temperature.

OVEN ROASTING: this method uses hot and dry air to surround the food, in an uncovered pan.

POT ROASTING: cooking meats by browning, and then cooking until tender, often with vegetables in a covered pot or Dutch oven.

STIR FRYING: this cooking method requires high heat, a little oil and continuous stirring.

PAN FRYING/PAN SEARING: cooking with small amounts of oil, on high heat, in a skillet to quickly create a crust that seals in meat juices.

MOIST-HEAT COOKING

BRAISING: this method involves first browning the meat in fat, and then simmering it in a small quantity of liquid in a covered container at relatively low temperatures for a long period of time.

STEWING: small or large pieces of meat, often with vegetables, are covered in liquid and simmered slowly in a tightly covered pan on the stove for a long period of time.

POACHING: the most gentle cooking method, poaching is when food is submerged in 160°F-180°F liquid and gently cooked until it is done.

STEAMING: this method is a very healthy way of cooking food; ingredients are placed on a rack over boiling water in a closed container.

BOILING: to cook food by immersion in boiling water, broth or other liquid; not recommended for meat or fish fillets, but can be a good choice for shellfish such as shrimp, crab and lobster.

A PROFESSIONAL CHEF IN HOT WATER (TRUE STORY)

I recently watched one of the top competitive cooking television shows and saw the best chef get eliminated. She had the finest presentation, but the judges didn't consider her efforts. She lost because she cut the fruit for her dessert on the same board on which she had previously prepared raw chicken. In her rush she had forgotten to properly clean the board, a mistake you can understand while a cook is under the pressure of the clock and the camera. She was devastated that she lost the championship.

That's my cautionary and inspirational way of telling you that clean-up is an important step in your cooking routine. I'm not talking about neatness. My kitchen is usually pretty disorganized so I can't give much advice in regards to having "everything in its place." Properly cleaning your surfaces and utensils has to become an automatic habit. It's a lot easier to do a little scrubbing than to wonder why someone in your family got sick from the lunch you made yesterday...

Luckily, there are all kinds of handy gadgets to help you. Try disposable cutting pads! Keep kitchen wipes handy! Make it a "you-ser" friendly atmosphere. Do your prep work close to the sink so rinsing and washing will be more automatic. CREATE THE HABIT and your family will adopt the habit of cleaning as well.

CLEAN: THIS SHOULD BE AN AUTOMATIC PART OF YOUR FOOD PREPARATION!

Wash hands and surfaces often with hot, soapy water. Washing your hands for 20 seconds or with an alcohol-based sanitizer is a good start. Don't forget to dry them as well with paper towels. A new research study shows that damp hands allow for bacteria to be transferred to other surfaces much more easily than dry hands! Who knew? (By the way, drying your hands on a dirty dish towel or the jeans you've been wearing all day doesn't count!)

Keep some good looking soap dispensers near the sink. Use pretty bottles and caps that pour (like the kind bars use for making drinks). If the soap is easy to reach it makes it easier to remember to keep washing up. If you have to bend down to the cabinet to get soap, you may just rinse your hands and cooking tools with water – and that's just not safe enough.

Wash cutting boards, dishes, utensils and counter tops with hot soapy water after preparing each food item. After your work area is clean, move on to the next food item.

SEPARATE: KEEP RAW MEAT, POULTRY, AND SEAFOOD FROM READY-TO-EAT FOODS (WATCH THOSE DRIPS!)

Always try to separate raw meat, poultry and seafood from other foods in your grocery shopping cart and in your refrigerator.

Use a different cutting board for raw meat – or at least scrub with hot, soapy water extra carefully.

Never place cooked food on an unwashed plate that previously held raw meat, poultry and seafood.

These are not old fashioned ideas. Forcing yourself to be more aware of separating foods will reduce the spread of germs. Cross-contamination is the scientific term for how bacteria can be spread from one food to another. Tummy ache is the non-scientific term for what happens if you take a chance and don't keep your kitchen clean.

TOO HOT? TOO COLD?

Pay close attention to food temperature. It's essential to keep track of the best temperature to serve your meat.

If you don't have a food thermometer, get one right away! Why guess when an easy-to-find, inexpensive tool can do the work for you? A digital thermometer is the snazziest and easiest to read—but use what you have and be sure that it's accurate. Find a "don't move" place to keep the thermometer. When things are getting hot you won't want to take the time to search. Be sure to clean the thermometer after each use.

You know that cooking times may vary. You should also know your stove and oven (and microwave and toaster oven) well so you can estimate how quickly or slowly things will cook. Thinner and thicker pans make a lot of difference as well.

Giving you one absolute temperature for each kind of food isn't practical because portion sizes can change the cooking time. Thinner meat cuts cook faster.

RECOMMENDED INTERNAL DONENESS TEMPERATURE

Insert your thermometer into the thickest part of the meat and poultry, making sure that the thermometer tip isn't touching any fat or bone. Take it out, read it and wash the thermometer so you don't have to rush to do it when you need it again.

Keep checking and cooking until you see the temperature that's just right for your specific cut of meat or seafood. You know that opinions about rare meat keep changing but the latest cooking regulations give you the idea of the temperatures you are trying to reach:

Whole cuts of beef and pork (including steaks, roasts, tenderloin and chops) have an internal doneness temperature of 145°F and should be left to rest for 3 minutes after being cooked.

Don't worry that your roast won't be hot because you "rest it" (let it sit before you slice and serve). The meat actually gets juicier and, since it's hot out of the oven, there's a little extra cooking going on while it's resting!

Ground beef and pork should be cooked to 160°F. Be particularly careful with these.

All poultry (and we mean the whole bird, various cuts or ground) should be cooked to a minimum of 165°F. Turkey burgers should be slightly more done than beef burgers.

Most cuts of fish are done if they flake easily when you test with a fork.

Shellfish is done when it looks more opaque (less transparent) and feels firm. Don't burn your fingers testing... the thermometer should be 145°F. Of course, the size and quantity means you have to check constantly.

Here is the internal temperature guideline for the different degrees of doneness for beef cuts:
- Medium Rare   145°F
- Medium   160°F
- Well-Done   170°F

Many thermometers have these numbers printed on them. You can also make yourself a little "cheat sheet" with the numbers you use the most and keep it near the thermometer. Wash the thermometer when you put it away! And it's not a waste of time to give it a rinse when you use it again.

CHILL OUT!

Cold temperatures keep harmful bacteria from growing and multiplying. Your kids know this from science class, but it's easy to take temperature for granted.

Set your refrigerator to a temperature no higher than 40°F and the freezer at 0°F or below.

Refrigerate or freeze perishables, prepared foods and leftovers no later than 2 hours after they have been prepared. You can put the platters in the fridge and then tidy things up later. It is not smart to leave food out while you are making dessert or enjoying all of the compliments and applause for your excellent cuisine.

Defrosting food at room temperature is really not the best method. Thaw it in the refrigerator. This process is slow, but it's safe! Make sure juices do not drip onto other foods or dishes in the refrigerator.

For faster defrosting, use your microwave oven. Make sure you set your microwave on the "Defrost" setting or at "50% Power." Remember, you don't want to start cooking when what you meant to do was defrost. Microwaves are speedy but you have to keep your eye on what you're defrosting at all times.

You can also defrost foods by placing your frozen protein in a leak-proof bag and submerging it in cold water. *Cold* water, not hot. It makes things go a little faster if you change the cold water every 30 minutes when you're defrosting raw meat, poultry and seafood.

Marinating meat can improve the flavor and texture. You can improvise a lot when you are marinating. But, don't let food sit on the counter while it's marinating. Cover and marinate foods in the refrigerator. You may use leftover marinade that was in contact with any raw meat, poultry or seafood **only if** you are going to use it for a sauce. However, you must first boil it to destroy any potentially harmful bacteria. Even better, save some unused marinade before placing raw meat, poultry, or seafood in it. The marinade on your meat will be safe because it is cooked and heated to the proper temperature. Heat all the marinade well that you've used to fix meat. Use it hot or just toss it.

notes

eating well

There's too much talk and too many arguments about what we should and should not eat. What's healthy, what's safe, and what's tempting are at the center of too many conversations!

You have to try to figure out what's good for you. Before you eat, think about what and how much food goes on your plate or in your cup or bowl. Throughout the day, include foods from all food groups: vegetables, fruits, whole grains, low-fat dairy products, and lean protein foods.

Here are some thoughts that seem to work:
- Make half of your plate fruits and vegetables.
- Make sure at least half of your grains are whole grain.
- Switch to non-fat or 1% milk.
- Vary your protein food choices.

This book will show you some widely accepted guidelines. If most of this information is stuff we've heard all of our lives, why do we eat poorly so much of the time? It takes effort and planning to choose and prepare healthy meals that are also yummy. We're just sayin', do some thinkin' along with your chewin'.

USDA's new MyPlate food guidance system is comprised of the new MyPlate symbol and other materials to help Americans make healthy food choices and to be active every day:

Protein Foods	Vegetables	Fruits	Grains	Dairy
Eat a variety of foods from the protein food group each week, such as: lean meats, poultry, seafood, eggs, beans and peas, as well as nuts. Twice a week, make seafood the protein on your plate. Choose lean meats and ground beef that's lean. Trim or drain fat from meat and remove skin from poultry to cut fat and calories.	Eat more red, orange, and dark-green veggies like tomatoes, sweet potatoes and broccoli in main dishes. Add beans or peas to salads (kidney or chickpeas), soups (split peas or lentils), and side dishes (pinto or baked beans), or serve as a main dish. Fresh, frozen, and canned vegetables all count. Choose "reduced sodium" or "no-salt-added" canned veggies.	Use fruits as snacks, salads, and desserts. At breakfast, top your cereal with bananas or strawberries; add blueberries to pancakes. Buy fruits that are dried, frozen, and canned (in water or 100% juice), as well as fresh fruits. Select 100% fruit juice when choosing juices.	Substitute whole-grain choices for refined-grain breads, bagels, rolls, breakfast cereals, crackers, rice, and pasta. Make sure at least half of your grains are whole grains. Check the ingredients list on product labels for the words "whole" or "whole grain" before the grain ingredient name. Choose products that name a whole grain first on the ingredients list.	Choose skim (fat-free) or 1% (low-fat) milk. They have the same amount of calcium and other essential nutrients as whole milk, but less fat and calories. Top fruit salads and baked potatoes with low-fat yogurt. If you are lactose intolerant, try lactose-free milk or fortified soymilk (soy beverage).
Eat 5½ ounces every day	**Eat 2½ cups every day**	**Eat 2 cups every day**	**Eat 6 ounces every day**	**Get 3 cups every day**
What counts as an ounce? 1 ounce of lean meat, poultry, or fish; 1 egg; 1 Tbsp peanut butter; ½ ounce nuts or seeds; ¼ cup beans or peas	What counts as a cup? 1 cup of raw or cooked vegetables or vegetable juice; 2 cups of leafy salad greens	What counts as a cup? 1 cup of raw or cooked fruit or 100% fruit juice; ½ cup dried fruit	What counts as an ounce? 1 slice of bread; ½ cup of cooked rice, cereal, or pasta; 1 ounce of ready-to-eat cereal	What counts as a cup? 1 cup of milk, yogurt, or fortified soymilk; 1½ ounces natural or 2 ounces processed cheese

Cut back on sodium and empty calories from solid fats and added sugars:

> Watch for salt content in the foods you buy. Compare sodium in foods and choose those with a lower number.
> Drink water instead of sugary drinks. Eat desserts full of sugar less often.
> Make foods that are high in solid fats - such as cakes, cookies, ice cream, pizza and cheese - occasional choices, not everyday foods.
> Limit empty calories to less than 260 calories per day based on a 2,000-calorie diet.

index

HOW MANY COOKS DOES IT TAKE TO BAKE A COOKBOOK?

Here's the Adam Taki special:

Start with a generous helping of my dad and best friend, Dr. Ghazi Taki – the recipe wouldn't work with out him.

Stir in Mom, Beverly Taki, to add love, support, and kitchen tricks.

Prepare in advance: Passion, Patience, Hard Work and a dish towel to mop up after the early under-baked batches.

Whip up a heap of advice and suggestions from Anna Ford.

You want to fold in spicy words from Jeanne Wolf.

Essential ingredients: Maureen Jones, Blake Knight, Dan Burton, Steve Lopez, Susan Turk, and Brittany Garrido.

Let Jeff Parker make the food look stylin' great so that Bobby Quillard can do the finish with some fabulous photos.

And you know what I'm going to say: Always reach for the Amazing Taste®.